MASTERING JAVASCRIPT

A Comprehensive Guide to Understanding JavaScript

ROWAN HAMPTON

TABLE OF CONTENTS

4

Introduction

Welcome to the world of JavaScript, a language that has transformed the landscape of web development and beyond. In today's digital age, JavaScript is not merely a scripting language confined to enhancing website interactivity; it has evolved into a versatile powerhouse driving the most innovative web applications, server-side technologies, mobile app development, and even desktop applications.

"Mastering JavaScript: A Comprehensive Guide" is your passport to unlocking the full potential of this dynamic and ubiquitous programming language. Whether you're a novice programmer taking your first steps into the world of coding or a seasoned developer seeking to refine your skills, this book is meticulously crafted to cater to your learning journey.

JavaScript's flexibility and ubiquity make it an essential skill for developers across various domains. With its roots firmly planted in the browser, JavaScript has transcended its origins to become a fundamental pillar of modern software development. From manipulating the Document Object Model (DOM) to creating interactive user interfaces, from handling asynchronous operations to building robust server-side applications, JavaScript empowers developers to bring their creative visions to life.

In this comprehensive guide, we will embark on a structured exploration of JavaScript's core concepts, advanced features, and best practices. From mastering the fundamentals of syntax and control flow to diving deep into object-oriented programming, asynchronous programming, and modern ES6+ features, each chapter is meticulously crafted to provide you with a solid foundation upon which to build your expertise.

Furthermore, we'll delve into practical real-world scenarios, such as working with APIs, testing and debugging applications, and exploring popular JavaScript frameworks and libraries. By the end of this journey, you will not only possess a deep understanding of JavaScript's intricacies but also the confidence to tackle any coding challenge that comes your way.

Whether your goal is to develop cutting-edge web applications, create dynamic user experiences, or embark on a career as a professional JavaScript developer, "Mastering JavaScript: A Comprehensive Guide" equips you with the knowledge, skills, and insights necessary to succeed in today's fast-paced tech industry.

So, without further ado, let's embark on this exhilarating journey into the heart of JavaScript mastery. Happy coding!

Chapter 1:
Getting Started with JavaScript

JavaScript is a versatile and powerful programming language that serves as the backbone of modern web development. In this chapter, we'll embark on our journey into the world of JavaScript by laying down the foundational concepts and skills necessary to kickstart your programming adventure.

1.1 Introduction to JavaScript:

JavaScript, often abbreviated as JS, was created by Brendan Eich in 1995 and initially intended to bring interactivity to web pages. Since then, it has grown exponentially in popularity and functionality, becoming an integral part of web development alongside HTML and CSS. Unlike its counterparts, JavaScript is a dynamic, object-oriented language with capabilities extending beyond client-side scripting to server-side development, mobile app development, game development, and more.

JavaScript's versatility stems from its ability to run in various environments, including web browsers, servers (via Node.js), and even mobile devices (via frameworks like React Native). This allows developers to leverage their JavaScript skills across different platforms and technologies, making it a valuable asset in today's software development landscape.

One of the key features of JavaScript is its event-driven nature, which allows developers to create interactive and responsive web applications. With JavaScript, you can listen for user interactions such as clicks, keyboard input, and mouse movements, and respond to them dynamically by updating the content or behavior of a web page in real-time.

JavaScript is also known for its flexibility and ease of use, thanks to its dynamic typing and lightweight syntax. This makes it accessible to beginners while still offering powerful features for more experienced developers. With JavaScript, you can manipulate HTML and CSS, interact with web APIs, perform asynchronous operations, and much more, all within a single programming language.

JavaScript is a versatile and powerful language that has revolutionized web development by enabling developers to create dynamic, interactive, and responsive web applications. In the following sections, we'll delve deeper into the core concepts of JavaScript and explore how you can leverage its capabilities to build modern web applications.

1.2 Setting Up Your Development Environment:

Before diving into writing JavaScript code, it's essential to set up your development environment. Fortunately, getting started with JavaScript requires minimal setup, as all you need is a text editor and a web browser. Popular text editors like Visual Studio Code, Sublime Text, or Atom provide a comfortable environment for writing and organizing your code. These editors offer features such as syntax highlighting, code completion, and customizable themes, making them ideal choices for JavaScript development.

Additionally, modern web browsers such as Google Chrome, Mozilla Firefox, or Microsoft Edge come equipped with built-in developer tools that aid in debugging and testing your JavaScript code. These developer tools offer a suite of features, including a JavaScript console for logging messages and errors, a DOM inspector for inspecting and modifying HTML elements, a network monitor for tracking HTTP requests and responses, and a debugger for stepping through JavaScript code line by line.

Furthermore, browser extensions like Redux DevTools, React Developer Tools, and Vue Devtools provide additional utilities for debugging and inspecting JavaScript code, particularly when working with specific frameworks like React or Vue.js.

In addition to text editors and web browsers, you may also consider installing Node.js, a JavaScript runtime environment that allows you to run JavaScript code outside of the browser, enabling server-side development and automation tasks. Node.js comes with npm (Node Package Manager), a package manager for installing and managing JavaScript libraries and tools.

Setting up a development environment for JavaScript is straightforward and flexible, allowing you to tailor it to your specific needs and preferences. Whether you're a beginner getting started with your first JavaScript project or an experienced developer working on a large-scale application, having the right tools and setup in place is essential for a smooth and productive development experience.

1.3 Basic Syntax and Structure:

JavaScript syntax is relatively straightforward and shares similarities with other programming languages like Java and C. A JavaScript program consists of a series of statements, each ending with a semicolon (;). This termination symbolizes the end of an instruction, helping the interpreter to understand where one statement ends and the next begins.

Comments play a crucial role in code documentation and readability. In JavaScript, single-line comments are denoted by two forward slashes (//), while multi-line comments are enclosed within /* and */. These annotations allow developers to explain their code, provide context, or disable specific portions temporarily.

Variables are fundamental constructs in JavaScript, used to store and manipulate data values. They are declared using the var, let, or const keywords, followed by a unique identifier (variable name). JavaScript variables can hold various types of data, including numbers, strings, booleans, arrays, and objects. Unlike some statically typed languages, JavaScript is dynamically typed, meaning variables can change types dynamically during execution.

For example:

```
// Declaring variables
var age = 25; // Number
var name = "John"; // String
var isStudent = true; // Boolean

// Changing variable types dynamically
var x = 5; // Number
x = "Hello"; // Now x is a String
```

JavaScript's loose typing allows for flexibility in coding but also requires careful attention to variable types to avoid unexpected behavior. While this dynamic nature can lead to more concise and expressive code, it also poses challenges in maintaining code integrity and debugging.

Understanding JavaScript syntax and the behavior of variables is essential for writing clean, efficient, and bug-free code. By mastering these foundational concepts, developers can unlock the full potential of JavaScript and build robust and scalable applications.

1.4 Variables, Data Types, and Operators:

Understanding variables, data types, and operators is fundamental to JavaScript programming. Variables serve as containers for storing data, and they can be declared using the keywords var, let, or const.

JavaScript supports several data types, each with its specific characteristics and uses. These data types include:

Numbers: Used to represent numeric values, both integers and floating-point numbers. For example:

```
var age = 25;
var price = 9.99;
```

Strings: Used to represent text data enclosed within single ('') or double ("") quotes. For example:

```
var name = 'John';
var message = "Hello, world!";
```

Booleans: Used to represent logical values, true or false. For example:

```
var isStudent = true;
var isLoggedIn = false;
```

Arrays: Used to store collections of data values, which can be of any data type, indexed by numerical positions starting from 0. For example:

```
var numbers = [1, 2, 3, 4, 5];
var colors = ['red', 'green', 'blue'];
```

Objects: Used to represent complex data structures consisting of key-value pairs, where keys are strings (properties) and values can be of any data type. For example:

```
var person = {
  name: 'John',
  age: 25,
  isStudent: true
};
```

JavaScript also supports other data types such as null and undefined, which represent the absence of a value or the lack of a defined value, respectively.

Operators are symbols used to perform operations on operands, which can be variables, constants, or literal values. JavaScript supports various types of operators, including:

Arithmetic operators (+, -, *, /, %): Used for basic arithmetic operations like addition, subtraction, multiplication, division, and modulus.

Comparison operators (==, ===, !=, !==, <, >, <=, >=): Used to compare two values and return a boolean result.

Logical operators (&&, ||, !): Used to perform logical operations such as AND, OR, and NOT on boolean values.

Understanding how to use variables, manipulate data types, and apply operators is essential for writing efficient and effective JavaScript code. By mastering these concepts, developers can create dynamic and interactive web applications with ease.

1.5 Control Flow and Loops:

Control flow statements allow you to control the execution flow of your JavaScript code based on conditions and loops. These statements enable you to make decisions and repeat actions, providing flexibility and control over the behavior of your programs.

Conditional statements, such as if...else and switch, enable you to execute different blocks of code depending on specified conditions. Conditional statements, such as if...else and else if, are essential tools in JavaScript for controlling the flow of execution based on specified conditions. These statements enable developers to create logic that responds dynamically to different scenarios, improving the flexibility and interactivity of their code.

With the if...else statement, you can execute a block of code if a condition is true, and an alternative block of code if the condition is false. The else if statement allows you to specify additional conditions to be evaluated if the initial condition is false but another condition is true.

In the provided example:

```
var age = 25;

if (age >= 18) {
  console.log("You are an adult.");
} else if (age >= 13) {
  console.log("You are a teenager.");
} else {
  console.log("You are a minor.");
}
```

The if...else statement first checks if the value of age is greater than or equal to 18. If true, it logs "You are an adult.". If false, it moves to the else if statement, which checks if the age is greater than or equal to 13. If true, it logs "You are a teenager.". If both conditions are false, it executes the else block and logs "You are a minor.".

By incorporating else if statements, developers can create more complex decision-making logic that considers multiple conditions, allowing for greater customization and adaptability in their JavaScript applications.

The switch statement provides an alternative way to handle multiple conditions more efficiently. It evaluates an expression and executes the corresponding block of code based on matching case values. For example:

```javascript
var day = 3;
var dayName;

switch (day) {
  case 1:
    dayName = "Monday";
    break;
  case 2:
    dayName = "Tuesday";
    break;
  case 3:
    dayName = "Wednesday";
    break;
  // More cases...
  default:
    dayName = "Unknown";
}
console.log("Today is " + dayName);
```

In the provided example, the variable day is assigned the value 3, representing Wednesday. The switch statement then evaluates the value of day and executes the corresponding block of code for the matching case value.

Since day is equal to 3, the case 3: is matched, and the variable dayName is assigned the value "Wednesday". The break statement is used to exit the switch statement after executing the corresponding block of code.

If day does not match any of the case values, the default case is executed. In this case, if day were assigned a value other than 1, 2, or 3, the variable dayName would be assigned the value "Unknown".

Using a switch statement in this scenario provides a cleaner and more concise way to handle multiple conditions compared to using multiple if...else statements. It also improves readability and maintainability, especially when dealing with a large number of possible case values.

Loops are essential constructs in JavaScript that allow you to repeat a block of code until a certain condition is met. JavaScript provides several types of loops, including for, while, and do...while, each with its own use cases and advantages.

The for loop is commonly used when you know the number of iterations in advance. It consists of three parts: an initialization, a condition, and an iteration statement. In the provided example:

```javascript
for (var i = 0; i < 5; i++) {
  console.log("Iteration " + i);
}
```

Here, the loop initializes a variable i to 0, checks if i is less than 5, and executes the block of code inside the loop. After each iteration, the value of i is incremented by 1 using the i++ statement. This loop will execute five times, logging "Iteration 0" through "Iteration 4" to the console.

The while loop is used when the number of iterations is not known in advance, but you want to continue looping until a condition is false. It consists of a single condition that is evaluated before each iteration. For example:

```
var i = 0;
while (i < 5) {
  console.log("Iteration " + i);
  i++;
}
```

In this example, the loop continues to execute as long as the condition i < 5 is true. Inside the loop, "Iteration 0" through "Iteration 4" are logged to the console, and i is incremented with each iteration until the condition becomes false.

The do...while loop is similar to the while loop, but it ensures that the block of code is executed at least once before checking the condition. For example:

```
var i = 0;
do {
  console.log("Iteration " + i);
  i++;
} while (i < 5);
```

In this case, the block of code inside the loop is executed first, regardless of the condition. Then, the loop continues to execute as long as the condition i < 5 is true. Like the while loop, "Iteration 0" through "Iteration 4" are logged to the console, and i is incremented with each iteration until the condition becomes false.

These loop constructs provide developers with powerful tools for iterating over data, performing repetitive tasks, and controlling the flow of execution in JavaScript applications. By understanding how to use loops effectively, you can write more efficient and concise code that accomplishes complex tasks with ease.

Mastering control flow and loops is essential for building dynamic and interactive JavaScript applications. By understanding how to use conditional statements and loops effectively, you can create code that responds to different scenarios and performs repetitive tasks efficiently, enhancing the functionality and user experience of your applications.

In this chapter, we've laid the groundwork for your JavaScript journey by introducing you to the language's fundamentals. As we progress through this book, we'll delve deeper into each concept, equipping you with the knowledge and skills necessary to become proficient in JavaScript development. So, let's roll up our sleeves and start coding!

Chapter 2:
Functions and Scope

Functions are the building blocks of JavaScript, allowing developers to encapsulate reusable blocks of code and execute them as needed. In this chapter, we'll delve into the intricacies of functions, exploring their various types, scopes, and advanced features.

2.1 Understanding Functions:

At its core, a function is a block of code designed to perform a specific task. Functions encapsulate a set of instructions, allowing you to reuse code and organize your program's logic effectively. In JavaScript, functions play a crucial role in creating modular and maintainable code.

Functions in JavaScript take inputs, known as parameters, and return outputs, referred to as return values. Parameters are variables that represent the inputs passed to a function, while return values are the results produced by the function after performing its task.

One of the key features of JavaScript is that functions are first-class citizens. This means that functions can be treated as values and manipulated just like any other data type. Specifically, functions can be assigned to variables, passed as arguments to other functions, and returned from other functions.

Let's consider a basic example of a function in JavaScript:

```
function greet(name) {
  return "Hello, " + name + "!";
}


console.log(greet("John")); // Output: Hello, John!
```

```

In this example, the `greet` function accepts a parameter `name`, representing the name of the person to greet. Inside the function, a greeting message is constructed using the provided name, and the message is returned as the output of the function.

The `console.log` statement demonstrates how we can call the `greet` function and pass it an argument ("John"). The function then executes, producing the greeting message "Hello, John!", which is logged to the console.

Functions are fundamental building blocks in JavaScript programming, enabling code reuse, abstraction, and modularity. By understanding how to define, call, and manipulate functions, you can write more efficient, organized, and maintainable code for your JavaScript applications.

## 2.2 Function Declarations vs. Function Expressions:

JavaScript provides two main ways to define functions: function declarations and function expressions. While both forms serve the same purpose of creating reusable blocks of code, they differ in their syntax, behavior, and usage.

### Function Declarations

Function declarations are defined using the function keyword followed by a name, a list of parameters enclosed in parentheses, and a block of code enclosed in curly braces. For example:

```
function add(a, b) {
  return a + b;
}
```

In function declarations, the function name is hoisted, meaning it can be called before its actual declaration in the code. This allows
```

you to define functions anywhere in your code, and they will still be accessible throughout the scope.

Function Expressions
Function expressions, on the other hand, define functions as values assigned to variables. They do not require a function name and are often assigned to variables using the assignment operator (=). For example:

```
const subtract = function(a, b) {
  return a - b;
};
```

In function expressions, the function is defined at the point where the variable is assigned. Unlike function declarations, function expressions are not hoisted. Therefore, they must be defined before they are called in the code.

Understanding the Differences
The key difference between function declarations and function expressions lies in their hoisting behavior and syntax. Function declarations are hoisted, making them accessible throughout their scope, while function expressions are not hoisted and must be defined before use.

Choosing between function declarations and function expressions depends on the specific requirements of your code. Function declarations are often preferred for their hoisting behavior and readability, especially for defining functions that need to be accessible across the entire scope. Function expressions, on the other hand, offer flexibility and can be used to create anonymous functions or functions that are only needed in a specific context.

Understanding the differences between function declarations and function expressions is crucial for writing clean, maintainable, and efficient JavaScript code. By choosing the appropriate form for defining functions based on your specific needs, you can improve the clarity and organization of your codebase.

2.3 Scope and Closures:

Scope refers to the visibility and accessibility of variables within a program. In JavaScript, variables can have either global scope, function scope, or block scope (introduced with let and const in ES6). Understanding scope is crucial for writing predictable and maintainable code, as it helps avoid variable conflicts and unintended side effects.

Global Scope

Variables declared outside of any function or block have global scope, meaning they can be accessed from anywhere within the program. While global variables provide convenience, they can also lead to namespace pollution and make it difficult to track variable usage.

```
var globalVariable = 'I am global';
```

Function Scope

Variables declared inside a function have function scope, meaning they are accessible only within that function. This helps encapsulate variables and prevents them from affecting other parts of the program.

```
function myFunction() {
  var localVar = 'I am local';
}
```

Block Scope

With the introduction of let and const in ES6, variables declared using these keywords have block scope, meaning they are accessible only within the block in which they are defined. This provides more fine-grained control over variable visibility and reduces the risk of unintended variable mutations.

```javascript
{
  let blockVar = 'I am block-scoped';
}
```

Closures

Closures occur when a function "remembers" its lexical scope even when executed outside that scope. This means that inner functions have access to the variables and parameters of their outer functions, even after the outer function has finished executing. Closures are a powerful feature of JavaScript and are commonly used to create private variables and maintain state in functional programming.

Here's an example demonstrating closures:

```javascript
function outer() {
  const message = 'Hello';

  function inner() {
    console.log(message);
  }

  return inner;
}

const innerFunction = outer();
innerFunction(); // Output: Hello
```

In this example, the inner function has access to the message variable declared in its outer function (outer), even though inner is executed outside of the outer function's scope. This is possible because of closures, which retain a reference to the variables of their outer lexical scope. Closures are particularly useful for creating modular and encapsulated code, allowing functions to maintain private state and behavior. Understanding closures and scope in JavaScript is essential for writing clean, efficient, and maintainable code.

2.4 Arrow Functions and Function Binding:

Arrow functions are a concise syntax introduced in ES6 for defining functions. They provide a more compact and readable way to write function expressions, particularly for simple, single-line functions.

Here's how you can rewrite the add function from earlier using an arrow function:

```
const add = (a, b) => a + b;
```

In this example, the arrow function (a, b) => a + b takes two parameters a and b, and returns their sum. Arrow functions eliminate the need for the function keyword and curly braces, resulting in cleaner and more concise code.

One of the key differences between arrow functions and regular functions is how they handle this. Arrow functions lexically bind the value of this, meaning they inherit the this value from their surrounding code. This behavior can lead to more predictable and intuitive this behavior, especially in nested functions or callback functions.

26

Function binding involves explicitly setting the value of this within a function. This is commonly necessary when dealing with object methods or callback functions, where the context of this needs to be controlled explicitly. Traditionally, developers have used methods like bind, call, or apply to achieve function binding.

Here's an example demonstrating function binding:

```
const person = {
  firstName: 'John',
  lastName: 'Doe',
  fullName: function() {
    return this.firstName + ' ' + this.lastName;
  }
};

const greeting = function() {
  return 'Hello, ' + this.fullName();
};

const boundGreeting = greeting.bind(person);

console.log(boundGreeting()); // Output: Hello, John Doe
```

In this example, the greeting function is defined to return a greeting message using the fullName method of the person object. However, since this within greeting is not bound to person, we use the bind method to explicitly set this to person. This ensures that greeting can access the fullName method of person correctly when called

However, arrow functions simplify function binding by automatically inheriting this from their lexical scope. This means that the value of this inside an arrow function is determined by the surrounding context where the arrow function is defined, rather than how it's called.

Advantages of Arrow Functions:
Concise Syntax:
Arrow functions allow you to write shorter and cleaner code, especially for simple, single-line functions. They eliminate the need for the function keyword and curly braces, resulting in more compact code.

Example:
```
// Traditional function
function double(x) {
  return x * 2;
}


// Arrow function
const double = x => x * 2;
```
Predictable this Behavior:
Arrow functions lexically bind the value of this, meaning they inherit the this value from their surrounding lexical scope. This ensures that this inside an arrow function refers to the this value of the enclosing context, providing more predictable behavior compared to regular functions.

Example:

```
javascript
Copy code
const obj = {
  value: 10,
  getValue: function() {
    return this.value;
  }
```

```javascript
};

// Using arrow function
const obj = {
  value: 10,
  getValue: () => this.value // 'this' refers to the global object
};
```

Limitations of Arrow Functions:
Cannot Be Used as Constructor Functions:
Arrow functions cannot be used as constructor functions to create new objects. They lack the prototype property and cannot be called with the new keyword, making them unsuitable for creating instances of objects.

Example:
```javascript
// Traditional constructor function
function Person(name) {
  this.name = name;
}
```

```javascript
// Arrow function cannot be used as constructor
const Person = name => {
  this.name = name; // Throws error
};
```

Lack of Arguments Object:
Arrow functions do not have their own arguments object. Instead, they inherit the arguments object from their containing lexical scope. This can lead to unexpected behavior when attempting to access arguments inside an arrow function.

Example:
```javascript
// Using arguments with a traditional function
```

```javascript
function sum() {
  let total = 0;
  for (let i = 0; i < arguments.length; i++) {
    total += arguments[i];
  }
  return total;
}


// Arrow function cannot access 'arguments'
const sum = () => {
  let total = 0;
  for (let i = 0; i < arguments.length; i++) { // 'arguments' is undefined
    total += arguments[i];
  }
  return total;
};
```

When to Use Arrow Functions:
For Short, Single-Line Functions:
Arrow functions are ideal for defining short, single-line functions, such as callbacks or concise utility functions. Their concise syntax improves code readability and reduces boilerplate.

When this Behavior Needs to Be Lexical:
Arrow functions are suitable for situations where you want this to be lexically bound, ensuring predictable behavior, especially in nested functions or callback functions.

When to Use Traditional Functions:
As Constructor Functions:
Traditional functions should be used when creating objects using the new keyword and prototype inheritance.

When Accessing arguments Object:
Traditional functions should be used when the function relies on the arguments object or requires its own arguments context.

Understanding the strengths and limitations of arrow functions versus traditional functions is crucial for writing efficient and maintainable JavaScript code. By choosing the appropriate type of function for each scenario, you can optimize code readability, performance, and maintainability in your projects.

2.5 IIFE (Immediately Invoked Function Expressions):

An Immediately Invoked Function Expression (IIFE) is a JavaScript function that is executed immediately after it is defined. This pattern is commonly used to create a private scope for variables and avoid polluting the global scope with unnecessary variables or functions.

Example of an IIFE:

```
(function() {
  var message = 'Hello, world!';
  console.log(message);
})();
```

In this example, an anonymous function is declared inside parentheses (function() { ... }) and immediately invoked (). This results in the function being executed immediately after it is defined. Inside the function, a variable message is declared and initialized with the string 'Hello, world!'. Finally, the message is logged to the console.

Benefits of Using IIFE:
Encapsulation:

IIFEs create a private scope for variables and functions, preventing them from polluting the global scope. This helps avoid naming conflicts and unintended variable modifications in larger applications.

Isolation:
By encapsulating code within an IIFE, you can isolate functionality and ensure that variables and functions defined within the IIFE do not interfere with other parts of the application. This promotes modularization and improves code maintainability.

Initialization:
IIFEs are often used for initializing variables, setting up configurations, or executing code that needs to run once when the script is loaded. This allows you to execute code immediately without waiting for an event or function call.

Common Use Cases of IIFE:
Module Pattern:
IIFEs are commonly used in conjunction with the module pattern to create encapsulated modules in JavaScript. This pattern allows you to define private variables and methods within a module while exposing only the necessary functionality to the outside world.

Immediately Executed Setup Code:
IIFEs are useful for executing setup code or initializing configurations when a script is loaded. This ensures that the setup code runs immediately without needing to wait for an explicit function call or event trigger.

Pollution Avoidance:
By encapsulating code within an IIFE, you can avoid polluting the global scope with unnecessary variables or functions. This helps

keep the global namespace clean and reduces the risk of naming conflicts in larger applications.

Overall, IIFEs are a powerful tool in JavaScript for creating private scopes, isolating functionality, and executing code immediately. They are commonly used in various design patterns and coding practices to improve code organization and maintainability.

Functions are the backbone of JavaScript, enabling developers to write modular, reusable code. By understanding the different types of functions, their scopes, and advanced features like closures and arrow functions, you can write more efficient and maintainable code. Additionally, mastering concepts like function binding and IIFEs will further enhance your JavaScript skills and enable you to tackle a wide range of programming challenges. As you continue your journey in JavaScript development, remember to practice these concepts regularly and explore their applications in real-world projects. Happy coding!

Chapter 3:
Working with Arrays and Objects

Arrays and objects are fundamental data structures in JavaScript, allowing developers to organize and manipulate data efficiently. In this chapter, we'll explore the intricacies of arrays and objects, including their manipulation, iteration, and the principles of object-oriented programming.

3.1 Arrays in JavaScript:

An array in JavaScript is a data structure that stores a collection of elements, each identified by an index. Arrays are dynamic, meaning they can grow or shrink in size as needed. They can store elements of any data type, including numbers, strings, booleans, objects, and even other arrays.

Creating Arrays:
You can create an array in JavaScript using square brackets [] notation or the Array constructor.

```
let numbers = [1, 2, 3, 4, 5];
let fruits = ['apple', 'banana', 'orange'];
```
Arrays can also be created using the Array constructor:

```
let numbers = new Array(1, 2, 3, 4, 5);
```

Accessing Array Elements:
Array elements are accessed using zero-based indices. You can access individual elements by specifying their index within square brackets [].

```
console.log(numbers[0]); // Output: 1
console.log(fruits[1]); // Output: 'banana'
```

Array Methods:
Arrays in JavaScript provide various built-in methods for manipulation, including adding or removing elements, sorting, searching, and iterating through elements.

```javascript
// Adding elements
numbers.push(6); // Adds 6 to the end of the array
fruits.unshift('grapes'); // Adds 'grapes' to the beginning of the array

// Removing elements
numbers.pop(); // Removes the last element from the array
fruits.shift(); // Removes the first element from the array

// Sorting elements
numbers.sort(); // Sorts the array in ascending order

// Searching elements
console.log(fruits.indexOf('banana')); // Returns the index of 'banana' in the array

// Iterating through elements
numbers.forEach(function(number) {
  console.log(number);
});
```

Common Array Operations:
Adding Elements:

push(): Adds elements to the end of an array.
unshift(): Adds elements to the beginning of an array.
Removing Elements:

pop(): Removes the last element from an array.

shift(): Removes the first element from an array.
Sorting Elements:

sort(): Sorts the elements of an array.
Searching Elements:

indexOf(): Returns the index of the first occurrence of a specified element in an array.
Iterating through Elements:

forEach(): Executes a provided function once for each array element.

Arrays are versatile and widely used in JavaScript for storing and manipulating collections of data. Understanding array methods and operations is essential for effective JavaScript programming.

3.2 Array Methods and Iteration:

JavaScript arrays provide a wide range of built-in methods for manipulating and iterating over array elements. These methods offer powerful functionality for adding, removing, and transforming elements within arrays. Understanding how to use these array methods is crucial for writing clean and efficient JavaScript code.

Commonly Used Array Methods:
push():

Adds one or more elements to the end of an array and returns the new length of the array.

```javascript
Copy code
let numbers = [1, 2, 3, 4, 5];
numbers.push(6); // numbers: [1, 2, 3, 4, 5, 6]
```

pop():

Removes the last element from an array and returns that element.
javascript
Copy code
```javascript
let numbers = [1, 2, 3, 4, 5];
let lastElement = numbers.pop(); // lastElement: 5, numbers: [1, 2, 3, 4]
```
shift():

Removes the first element from an array and returns that element. The remaining elements' indices are updated.
javascript
Copy code
```javascript
let numbers = [1, 2, 3, 4, 5];
let firstElement = numbers.shift(); // firstElement: 1, numbers: [2, 3, 4, 5]
```
unshift():

Adds one or more elements to the beginning of an array and returns the new length of the array.
javascript
Copy code
```javascript
let numbers = [2, 3, 4, 5];
numbers.unshift(1); // numbers: [1, 2, 3, 4, 5]
```
splice():

Changes the contents of an array by removing or replacing existing elements and/or adding new elements in place.
javascript
Copy code
```javascript
let numbers = [1, 2, 3, 4, 5];
numbers.splice(2, 1, 'a', 'b'); // numbers: [1, 2, 'a', 'b', 4, 5]
```
slice():

Returns a shallow copy of a portion of an array into a new array object selected from start to end.

```
let numbers = [1, 2, 3, 4, 5];
let slicedArray = numbers.slice(2); // slicedArray: [3, 4, 5]
```

concat(): Combines two or more arrays and returns a new array.

```
let numbers1 = [1, 2];
let numbers2 = [3, 4, 5];
let combinedArray = numbers1.concat(numbers2);
// combinedArray: [1, 2, 3, 4, 5]
```

indexOf(): Returns the first index at which a given element can be found in the array, or -1 if it is not present.

```
let fruits = ['apple', 'banana', 'orange'];
let index = fruits.indexOf('banana'); // index: 1
```

forEach(): Executes a provided function once for each array element.

```
let numbers = [1, 2, 3, 4, 5];
numbers.forEach(num => console.log(num));
```

map(): Creates a new array populated with the results of calling a provided function on every element in the calling array.

```
let numbers = [1, 2, 3, 4, 5];
let squaredNumbers = numbers.map(num => num * num);
// squaredNumbers: [1, 4, 9, 16, 25]
```

filter(): Creates a new array with all elements that pass the test implemented by the provided function.

```
let numbers = [1, 2, 3, 4, 5];
let evenNumbers = numbers.filter(num => num % 2 === 0);
// evenNumbers: [2, 4]
```

reduce(): Executes a reducer function on each element of the array, resulting in a single output value.

```
let numbers = [1, 2, 3, 4, 5];
let sum = numbers.reduce((accumulator, currentValue) => accumulator + currentValue); // sum: 15
```

These array methods provide essential functionality for working with arrays in JavaScript. By leveraging these methods effectively, you can perform a wide range of operations on arrays, making your code more expressive and efficient.

3.3 Understanding Objects:

Objects in JavaScript are collections of key-value pairs, where each key is a string (or symbol) and each value can be of any data type. They are versatile data structures that allow you to represent complex entities and organize related data efficiently. Objects can contain nested objects, arrays, functions, and other primitive data types.

Creating Objects:
You can create an object in JavaScript using object literal notation:

```
let person = {
 name: 'John Doe',
 age: 30,
 address: {
```

```
    street: '123 Main St',
    city: 'New York',
    country: 'USA'
  }
};
```

This creates an object named person with three properties: name, age, and address. The address property itself is an object containing its own properties.

Accessing Object Properties:
You can access properties of an object using dot notation or bracket notation:

```
console.log(person.name); // Output: John Doe
console.log(person.address.city); // Output: New York
or

console.log(person['name']); // Output: John Doe
console.log(person['address']['city']); // Output: New York
```

Both methods yield the same result, allowing you to retrieve values associated with specific keys within the object.

Objects as Versatile Data Structures:
Objects are highly versatile and can represent various data structures, including:

Nested Objects: Objects can contain other objects as properties, allowing you to create hierarchical data structures.

Arrays: Objects can contain arrays as properties, enabling you to store collections of data.

Functions: Objects can contain functions as properties, allowing you to encapsulate behavior within an object.

Primitive Data Types: Objects can store primitive data types such as strings, numbers, booleans, and symbols.

Object Methods:
JavaScript objects provide a range of built-in methods for manipulating and interacting with them. These methods offer powerful functionality for iterating over object properties, extracting keys and values, and performing various operations on objects. Understanding and utilizing these methods is essential for effective object manipulation in JavaScript.

Commonly Used Object Methods:

Object.keys(): Returns an array of a given object's own enumerable property names.

```
const person = { name: 'John', age: 30, city: 'New York' };
const keys = Object.keys(person); // keys: ['name', 'age', 'city']
```

Object.values(): Returns an array of a given object's own enumerable property values.

```
const person = { name: 'John', age: 30, city: 'New York' };
const values = Object.values(person); // values: ['John', 30, 'New York']
```

Object.entries(): Returns an array of a given object's own enumerable property key-value pairs, in the form of an array.

```
const person = { name: 'John', age: 30, city: 'New York' };
const entries = Object.entries(person);
```

```javascript
// entries: [['name', 'John'], ['age', 30], ['city', 'New York']]
```

Object.assign(): Copies the values of all enumerable own properties from one or more source objects to a target object.

```javascript
const target = { a: 1, b: 2 };
const source = { b: 4, c: 5 };
const merged = Object.assign(target, source);
// merged: { a: 1, b: 4, c: 5 }
```

Object.freeze(): Freezes an object: other code cannot delete or change its properties.

```javascript
const person = { name: 'John', age: 30 };
Object.freeze(person);
person.age = 40; // This change will not take effect as the object is frozen.
```

Object.seal(): Prevents new properties from being added to an object and marks all existing properties as non-configurable.

```javascript
const person = { name: 'John', age: 30 };
Object.seal(person);
person.city = 'New York';
// This addition will not take effect as the object is sealed.
```

These built-in methods provide convenient ways to manipulate and interact with JavaScript objects. By leveraging these methods effectively, you can efficiently work with objects, extract necessary information, and perform various operations to meet your application's requirements..

Objects provide a convenient way to organize and access related data in JavaScript. They are widely used in JavaScript applications for representing real-world entities, managing state, and structuring data efficiently. Understanding how to work with objects is essential for mastering JavaScript programming.

3.4 Object-Oriented Programming in JavaScript:

JavaScript is a versatile language that supports both procedural and object-oriented programming paradigms. Object-oriented programming (OOP) is a programming paradigm centered around the concept of "objects," which encapsulate both data and behavior.

Creating Objects in JavaScript:
JavaScript offers various ways to create objects. One common approach is using constructor functions, which serve as blueprints for creating multiple instances of objects with similar properties and methods.

```
function Person(name, age) {
  this.name = name;
  this.age = age;
}

let john = new Person('John Doe', 30);
console.log(john.name); // Output: John Doe
console.log(john.age); // Output: 30
```

In this example, the Person constructor function defines properties for a person's name and age. We then create a new Person object named john using the new keyword.

Prototypes and Inheritance:
JavaScript utilizes prototypal inheritance to enable object reuse and inheritance. Every JavaScript object has a prototype, which serves as a template for properties and methods. When accessing

a property or method on an object, JavaScript first checks if the object itself has that property or method. If not, it traverses up the prototype chain until it finds the property or method or reaches the end of the chain (Object.prototype).

```javascript
function Animal(name) {
  this.name = name;
}

Animal.prototype.sayName = function() {
  console.log('My name is ' + this.name);
};

function Dog(name, breed) {
  Animal.call(this, name);
  this.breed = breed;
}

Dog.prototype = Object.create(Animal.prototype);
Dog.prototype.constructor = Dog;

let dog = new Dog('Buddy', 'Golden Retriever');
dog.sayName(); // Output: My name is Buddy
```

In this example, we define an Animal constructor function with a method sayName. We then create a Dog constructor function that inherits properties and methods from Animal. By setting Dog.prototype to an instance of Animal.prototype, we establish a prototype chain, allowing instances of Dog to access methods defined in Animal.

Understanding object-oriented programming concepts like constructors, prototypes, and inheritance is essential for creating reusable and maintainable JavaScript code. These concepts enable you to model real-world entities effectively and organize your code in a structured manner.

Arrays and objects are essential components of JavaScript, providing developers with powerful tools for organizing and manipulating data. By mastering arrays, objects, and object-oriented programming concepts like prototypes and inheritance, you'll be better equipped to build complex and scalable applications. As you continue your journey in JavaScript development, remember to practice these concepts regularly and explore their applications in real-world projects. Happy coding!

Chapter 4:
DOM Manipulation and Events

The Document Object Model (DOM) serves as a structured representation of HTML documents, enabling JavaScript to interact with and manipulate web page content dynamically. In this chapter, we delve into the fundamentals of DOM manipulation and event handling, essential skills for building dynamic and interactive web applications.

4.1 Introduction to the Document Object Model (DOM)

The Document Object Model (DOM) serves as a crucial bridge between web documents and JavaScript, providing a structured representation of HTML documents that JavaScript can interact with dynamically. Essentially, the DOM presents HTML documents as a hierarchical tree-like structure, where each element, attribute, or text node in the HTML document is represented as a node in the tree.

JavaScript leverages the DOM to access, modify, and manipulate web page content in real-time. Developers can utilize JavaScript to traverse the DOM tree, locating specific elements or nodes, and then apply changes to their attributes, content, or styles dynamically. This interaction with the DOM enables developers to create dynamic and interactive web experiences by updating page content based on user actions, application logic, or external events.

By leveraging the DOM's tree structure, developers can respond to user interactions, such as clicks or keyboard inputs, by modifying specific elements or updating their appearance. Additionally, developers can create interactive forms, validate user inputs, and dynamically load content from external sources by manipulating the DOM in response to various events.

Overall, the DOM serves as a fundamental mechanism for JavaScript to interact with web documents, enabling developers to create dynamic and responsive web applications that engage users and deliver seamless user experiences. Understanding how to effectively utilize the DOM empowers developers to build modern web applications that adapt to user interactions and deliver rich, interactive content.

4.2 Selecting DOM Elements

Selecting DOM elements is a crucial step in DOM manipulation, as it allows developers to target specific elements within a web page for further interaction and modification using JavaScript. JavaScript provides several methods and techniques for selecting DOM elements based on different criteria such as IDs, classes, tags, attributes, and more.

One of the most basic methods for selecting DOM elements is getElementById(), which retrieves an element based on its unique ID attribute. This method is commonly used when developers need to access a specific element with a known ID.

Another commonly used method is getElementsByClassName(), which retrieves a collection of elements that have the same class name. This method is useful when developers want to target multiple elements with the same class for manipulation.

Similarly, getElementsByTagName() retrieves a collection of elements with the specified tag name, allowing developers to target all elements of a particular type, such as <div>, <p>, or <a>.

For more precise selection, developers can use querySelector() and querySelectorAll() methods. querySelector() returns the first element that matches a specified CSS selector, while querySelectorAll() returns a collection of all elements that match the selector. These methods offer powerful capabilities for targeting elements based on complex CSS selectors, IDs, classes, attributes, and more.

Overall, the ability to select DOM elements efficiently is essential for effective DOM manipulation in JavaScript. By leveraging these selection methods, developers can precisely target elements within a web page and perform various actions such as updating content, modifying styles, adding event listeners, and more, thereby creating dynamic and interactive web experiences.

4.3 Modifying DOM Elements

Once DOM elements are selected, developers have the ability to dynamically modify various aspects of these elements using JavaScript. This dynamic modification enables the creation of interactive and responsive user interfaces, where elements can update in real-time based on user interactions or application logic.

Some common tasks involved in modifying DOM elements include:

Changing Text Content: JavaScript allows developers to update the text content of HTML elements dynamically. This can be achieved by accessing the textContent property of the selected element and assigning it a new value.

Updating Attribute Values: DOM elements often have attributes such as src, href, id, class, etc. JavaScript enables developers to modify these attributes dynamically by accessing them directly through the element's properties, such as element.src, element.href, etc.

Adding or Removing Classes: Classes play a crucial role in styling elements using CSS. JavaScript provides methods such as classList.add() and classList.remove() to add or remove classes from DOM elements dynamically, thereby changing their appearance or behavior.

Manipulating Styles: Developers can modify the inline styles of DOM elements directly using JavaScript. This can be achieved by accessing the style property of the element and assigning new CSS styles to it.

Appending or Removing Elements: JavaScript allows developers to add new elements to the DOM tree dynamically or remove existing ones. This can be accomplished using methods such as appendChild(), removeChild(), insertBefore(), etc.

By leveraging these techniques, developers can create dynamic and interactive user interfaces that respond to user actions or application events. Whether it's updating the content of a webpage, modifying the appearance of elements, or adding/removing elements dynamically, JavaScript provides powerful capabilities for modifying DOM elements and creating engaging user experiences.

4.4 Handling Events

Event handling is a fundamental aspect of web development, allowing developers to create interactive and responsive web applications by responding to user interactions such as clicks, mouse movements, keyboard inputs, and form submissions. JavaScript provides powerful mechanisms for handling events, enabling developers to register event listeners on DOM elements and execute callback functions in response to specific events.

Using event listeners, developers can attach event handlers to DOM elements using methods like addEventListener(). These event handlers listen for specific events, such as clicks or keypresses, and execute designated callback functions when those events occur.

This allows developers to define custom behavior for various user actions, such as validating form inputs, navigating through a slideshow, or updating content dynamically.

Event handling plays a crucial role in creating engaging user experiences and enhancing user engagement on web applications. By responding to user interactions in real-time, developers can create interfaces that feel intuitive and responsive, leading to a more enjoyable and interactive user experience. Whether it's implementing interactive features, validating user input, or triggering animations, event handling is an essential part of building modern web applications.

4.5 Event Bubbling and Event Delegation

Event bubbling and event delegation are important concepts in event handling that influence how events propagate through the Document Object Model (DOM) tree and how event handlers are managed.

Event bubbling refers to the natural propagation of an event from the target element on which the event occurred up through its ancestors in the DOM hierarchy. When an event occurs on an element, such as a click event, it triggers event handlers attached to that element first. Then, the event bubbles up through the parent elements, triggering event handlers on each ancestor element along the way until it reaches the root element or encounters a handler that stops propagation using the stopPropagation() method.

Event bubbling is beneficial because it allows you to attach event handlers to parent elements rather than individual child elements, making event management more efficient and reducing the need for excessive event listeners. It simplifies event handling and promotes cleaner code organization by centralizing event logic.

Event delegation is a technique used to handle events on multiple child elements by attaching a single event listener to a common ancestor element. When an event occurs on a descendant element, such as a button within a list, the event bubbles up to the ancestor element where the event listener is attached. The event handler then checks the event target to determine which specific child element triggered the event and executes the appropriate action based on the target element.

Event delegation is particularly useful for scenarios involving dynamically created elements or nested structures where adding individual event listeners to each element would be impractical or inefficient. By leveraging event delegation, you can simplify event management, improve performance, and ensure that dynamically added elements are also covered by event handling logic.

Overall, understanding event bubbling and event delegation is essential for effective event handling in JavaScript applications. By utilizing these concepts appropriately, developers can create more efficient, scalable, and maintainable event-driven applications.

In this chapter, we explore the principles of DOM manipulation and event handling, equipping developers with the knowledge and skills to create dynamic, interactive, and responsive web applications. Understanding the DOM and mastering event handling are essential for building modern web experiences that engage users and deliver compelling user interfaces.

Chapter 5:
Asynchronous JavaScript

Asynchronous JavaScript programming is fundamental for building responsive and efficient web applications. In this chapter, we'll explore the concepts and techniques behind asynchronous programming in JavaScript, including callbacks, promises, async/await, and working with asynchronous operations such as fetching data from APIs.

5.1 Understanding Asynchronous Programming:

In JavaScript, code execution is typically synchronous, meaning statements are executed line by line, and each statement must wait for the previous one to finish before executing. However, in asynchronous programming, certain operations can be initiated without waiting for their completion. Instead, they execute in the background, and their results are handled later.

Importance of Asynchronous Programming:
Asynchronous programming is crucial for various tasks such as:

Fetching Data from Servers:
When fetching data from servers, such as making HTTP requests, it's essential not to block the execution of other code while waiting for the response. Asynchronous operations allow you to initiate the request and continue executing other tasks. Once the response is received, a callback function or a promise can handle the data.
Handling User Interactions:

In web development, handling user interactions like button clicks, form submissions, or mouse movements asynchronously ensures that the application remains responsive. Instead of freezing the UI

while waiting for a response, asynchronous operations allow the interface to remain interactive.
Executing Time-Consuming Operations Efficiently:

Asynchronous programming enables the execution of time-consuming operations, such as image processing or file I/O, without blocking the main thread. By offloading these tasks to background threads or utilizing non-blocking I/O operations, the application can remain responsive and handle multiple tasks simultaneously.
Asynchronous Programming Techniques:
JavaScript offers several techniques for asynchronous programming, including:

Callbacks:
Callback functions are a traditional asynchronous programming technique in JavaScript. They allow you to specify a function to be executed once an asynchronous operation completes.
Promises:

Promises provide a more structured and flexible approach to handling asynchronous operations. They represent a value that may be available now, or in the future, or never. Promises allow chaining multiple asynchronous operations together and handling errors more effectively.
Async/Await:

Async functions and the await keyword provide a more readable and concise syntax for working with asynchronous code. Async functions return a promise implicitly, and the await keyword pauses the execution of the function until the promise is resolved or rejected.

Asynchronous programming is a fundamental aspect of modern JavaScript development, enabling efficient handling of tasks that involve waiting for external resources or time-consuming operations. Understanding and mastering asynchronous programming techniques are essential skills for building responsive, scalable, and performant JavaScript applications.

5.2 Callbacks and Callback Hell:

Callbacks are a common pattern used in JavaScript for handling asynchronous operations. A callback is a function passed as an argument to another function, which is invoked once the asynchronous operation completes.

Handling Asynchronous Code with Callbacks:
Here's an example of using callbacks to handle asynchronous code:

```javascript
function fetchData(callback) {
  setTimeout(() => {
    callback('Data fetched successfully');
  }, 1000);
}

fetchData((data) => {
  console.log(data); // Output: Data fetched successfully
});
```

In this example, the fetchData function simulates an asynchronous operation using setTimeout. Once the operation completes, it invokes the callback function with the fetched data.

Callback Hell:
However, nesting multiple callbacks can lead to a phenomenon known as "callback hell," where code becomes difficult to read and maintain due to excessive indentation and nested callbacks.

```javascript
asyncFunction1(() => {
```

```
  asyncFunction2(() => {
    asyncFunction3(() => {
      // More nested callbacks...
    });
  });
});
```

This nested callback structure can quickly become unwieldy and challenging to manage, especially as the number of asynchronous operations increases.

Limitations of Callbacks:
Callbacks have several limitations, including:

Readability and Maintainability:
Nested callbacks can lead to unreadable and difficult-to-maintain code, making it hard to understand the flow of execution.

Error Handling:
Error handling in callback-based code can become cumbersome, as each callback needs to handle its own errors, leading to repetitive error-handling logic.

Callback Hell:
As mentioned earlier, nesting multiple callbacks can result in callback hell, making the codebase hard to manage.

While callbacks are a fundamental asynchronous programming technique in JavaScript, they have limitations that can make code harder to maintain and understand. Asynchronous programming has evolved with the introduction of promises and async/await, offering more structured and readable alternatives for handling asynchronous code. However, understanding callbacks is still essential for working with older codebases and legacy APIs.

5.3 Promises and Promise Chaining:

Promises were introduced in ES6 as a cleaner alternative to callbacks for handling asynchronous operations. A promise represents a value that may be available now, or in the future, or never.

Creating and Using Promises:
Here's how you can create and use promises in JavaScript:

```
const fetchData = new Promise((resolve, reject) => {
  setTimeout(() => {
    resolve('Data fetched successfully');
  }, 1000);
});

fetchData.then((data) => {
  console.log(data); // Output: Data fetched successfully
}).catch((error) => {
  console.error(error);
});
```

In this example, we create a new promise using the Promise constructor. Inside the constructor, we define an asynchronous operation, such as fetching data after a timeout. If the operation is successful, we call the resolve function with the fetched data. Otherwise, if an error occurs, we call the reject function with the error.

We then use the .then() method to handle the resolved value (data) and the .catch() method to handle any errors that occur during the asynchronous operation.

Promise Chaining:

Promise chaining allows you to perform multiple asynchronous operations sequentially. Each .then() call returns a new promise, allowing you to chain multiple asynchronous operations together.

```
fetchData()
  .then((data) => processData(data))
  .then((result) => displayResult(result))
  .catch((error) => handleError(error));
```

In this example, fetchData() returns a promise. We chain multiple .then() calls to process the data returned by each asynchronous operation sequentially. If any error occurs during the chain, it is caught by the .catch() method.

Benefits of Promises:
Readability:

Promises offer cleaner and more readable code compared to nested callbacks, making it easier to understand the flow of asynchronous operations.
Error Handling:

Promises provide built-in error handling through the .catch() method, simplifying error management in asynchronous code.
Promise Chaining:

Promise chaining allows for sequential execution of asynchronous operations, improving code organization and readability.
Conclusion:
Promises are a powerful tool for handling asynchronous operations in JavaScript. They provide a cleaner and more structured approach compared to callbacks, enabling better error handling and promise chaining. Promises are widely used in modern JavaScript

development and are essential for writing efficient and maintainable asynchronous code.

5.4 Async/Await:

Async/await is a syntactic sugar built on top of promises, introduced in ES8. It provides a more concise and readable way to write asynchronous code, avoiding the need for explicit promise chaining or nested callbacks.

Using Async/Await:
Here's how you can rewrite the previous example using async/await:

```javascript
async function fetchData() {
  return new Promise((resolve) => {
   setTimeout(() => {
    resolve('Data fetched successfully');
   }, 1000);
  });
}

async function fetchDataAndProcess() {
  try {
   const data = await fetchData();
   console.log(data); // Output: Data fetched successfully
  } catch (error) {
   console.error(error);
  }
}

fetchDataAndProcess();
```

In this example, fetchData() is an async function that returns a promise. Inside fetchDataAndProcess(), we use the await keyword to pause the execution of the function until the promise returned by fetchData() resolves. Once the promise resolves, the value is assigned to the data variable, and we can proceed with further processing. If an error occurs during the asynchronous operation, it is caught by the try/catch block.

Benefits of Async/Await:
Readability:
Async/await syntax makes asynchronous code more readable and easier to understand compared to traditional promise chaining or nested callbacks.

Conciseness:
Async/await allows you to write asynchronous code in a synchronous style, reducing the need for boilerplate code and improving code expressiveness.

Error Handling:
Async/await simplifies error handling by allowing you to use try/catch blocks around asynchronous operations, making error management more intuitive.

Using .then() and .catch() with Async Functions:
Async functions return a promise, allowing you to use .then() and .catch() to handle success and error conditions:

```
fetchDataAndProcess()
  .then(() => {
   // Success handling
  })
  .catch((error) => {
   // Error handling
  });
```

This approach is useful when you need to handle success and error conditions separately or when integrating async functions with existing promise-based code.

Async/await is a powerful feature in JavaScript for writing asynchronous code in a more synchronous and readable manner. It simplifies error handling and makes asynchronous code easier to reason about, leading to more maintainable and efficient applications. Async/await is widely adopted in modern JavaScript development and is considered the preferred approach for handling asynchronous operations.

5.5 Working with Fetch API:

The Fetch API provides a modern interface for fetching resources asynchronously over the network. It is commonly used in web development to interact with APIs, fetch data from servers, and perform AJAX requests. Let's delve into the details of working with the Fetch API:

Making a Fetch Request:
To initiate a fetch request, you use the fetch() function, passing it the URL of the resource you want to fetch. Here's an example of making a basic GET request:

Here's how you can use the Fetch API to fetch data from a remote server:

```javascript
fetch('https://api.example.com/data')
  .then((response) => response.json())
  .then((data) => {
   console.log(data);
  })
  .catch((error) => {
   console.error(error);
```

  });

In this example:

We use the fetch() function to initiate an HTTP GET request to the
specified URL (https://api.example.com/data).
The fetch() function returns a promise that resolves to the
Response object representing the response to the request.
We use the .then() method to handle the response asynchronously.
Inside the first .then() callback, we use the response.json() method
to parse the JSON content of the response.
The parsed JSON data is then available in the second .then()
callback, where we can process and use it as needed.
Any errors that occur during the fetch operation are caught and
handled in the .catch() block.

Handling the Response:
The fetch() function returns a promise that resolves to a Response
object representing the response to the request. You can use the
.then() method to handle the response asynchronously. Inside the
.then() callback, you can access properties and methods of the
Response object to process the response data.

Parsing Response Data:
Often, the response contains data in JSON format. You can use the
.json() method to parse the JSON content of the response and work
with it as JavaScript objects. Here's how you can parse JSON
response data:

```javascript
fetch('https://api.example.com/data')
  .then((response) => response.json())
  .then((data) => {
    // Process the JSON data
  })
```

```
  .catch((error) => {
    // Handle any errors
  });
```

Customizing Fetch Requests:
You can customize fetch requests by providing additional options such as request method, headers, body, and more. For example, to make a POST request with custom headers and request body:

```
fetch('https://api.example.com/postData', {
  method: 'POST',
  headers: {
    'Content-Type': 'application/json',
    'Authorization': 'Bearer token'
  },
  body: JSON.stringify({ key: 'value' })
})
.then((response) => {
  // Handle the response
})
.catch((error) => {
  // Handle any errors
});
```

Error Handling:
It's essential to handle errors that may occur during the fetch operation. You can use the .catch() method to catch and handle any errors that occur during the fetch request:

```
fetch('https://api.example.com/data')
  .then((response) => {
    // Handle the response
  })
  .catch((error) => {
```

```javascript
    // Handle any errors
    console.error(error);
  });
```

The Fetch API provides a modern and versatile way to fetch resources asynchronously over the network. By understanding how to make fetch requests, handle responses, parse data, customize requests, and handle errors, you can effectively work with the Fetch API in your JavaScript applications to fetch data from servers, interact with APIs, and perform various HTTP-based interactions.

Asynchronous JavaScript programming is essential for building modern web applications that are responsive and efficient. By understanding concepts like callbacks, promises, async/await, and working with asynchronous operations like the Fetch API, you can write cleaner, more maintainable code that handles asynchronous tasks effectively. As you continue your journey in JavaScript development, remember to practice these concepts regularly and explore their applications in real-world projects. Happy coding!

Chapter 6:
ES6+ Features and Beyond

JavaScript has evolved significantly over the years, introducing new features and enhancements to improve the developer experience and the language's capabilities. In this chapter, we'll explore some of the key features introduced in ECMAScript 6 (ES6) and beyond, including arrow functions, template literals, destructuring, spread/rest operators, classes, modules, and new data structures like sets and maps.

6.1 Overview of ES6 Features:

ECMAScript 6, commonly referred to as ES6 or ES2015, revolutionized the landscape of JavaScript development by introducing a plethora of powerful enhancements and syntax improvements. This milestone release addressed many longstanding limitations and inconsistencies in the language, providing developers with a more modern and expressive toolset. Some of the standout features introduced in ES6 include arrow functions, template literals, destructuring, let and const for variable declarations, classes, and modules.

Arrow functions are perhaps one of the most impactful additions to JavaScript syntax. They offer a concise and more readable way to define functions, especially for short, one-line expressions. Arrow functions also provide lexical scoping for the this keyword, eliminating the need for developers to manually bind context within callback functions.

Template literals, another key feature of ES6, vastly improve string manipulation and interpolation in JavaScript. With template literals, developers can easily embed expressions and variables within strings using ${}, resulting in cleaner and more maintainable code compared to traditional string concatenation methods.

Destructuring enables developers to extract values from arrays or objects and assign them to variables in a succinct and intuitive manner. This feature simplifies code by reducing redundancy and improving readability, particularly in scenarios involving complex data structures.

The introduction of let and const for variable declarations brought much-needed clarity and consistency to variable scoping in JavaScript. Unlike var, which is function-scoped, let and const are block-scoped, providing better control over variable lifetimes and reducing the risk of unintended side effects.

ES6 also standardized class syntax, making it easier for developers familiar with object-oriented programming to create and work with classes and objects in JavaScript. The class keyword provides a more structured and intuitive way to define constructor functions and prototype-based inheritance.

Additionally, ES6 introduced native support for modules, allowing developers to organize code into reusable and encapsulated units. Modules promote modularity, encapsulation, and dependency management, facilitating better code organization and maintainability in large-scale applications.

Overall, ECMAScript 6 ushered in a new era of JavaScript development, empowering developers with a more modern, expressive, and consistent language foundation. The features introduced in ES6 have since become integral parts of the JavaScript ecosystem, shaping the way developers write and maintain code in both frontend and backend environments.

Arrow functions, introduced in ECMAScript 6 (ES6), offer a concise and elegant syntax for defining functions in JavaScript. They provide a more compact alternative to traditional function expressions, making code easier to read and write. One of the key advantages of arrow functions is their automatic lexical binding of the this keyword, which eliminates the need for developers to manually bind context within callback functions and event handlers. This behavior simplifies code and reduces the potential for errors, especially in complex scenarios where the context of this can be ambiguous.

Template literals, another feature introduced in ES6, revolutionized string manipulation and interpolation in JavaScript. They allow developers to create more expressive and readable strings by embedding expressions and variables directly within the string using ${} placeholders. This feature enables dynamic string construction with minimal concatenation, resulting in cleaner and more maintainable code. Additionally, template literals support multiline strings, making it easier to represent text blocks that span multiple lines without the need for escaping characters like newline (\n) or concatenation.

Here's an example showcasing both arrow functions and template literals:

```javascript
// Arrow function example
const greet = (name) => {
  return `Hello, ${name}!`;
};


// Template literal example
const user = { name: 'John' };
const message = `Welcome to our website, ${user.name}!`;
```

In this example, the greet function uses an arrow function to define a concise greeting message, while the message variable employs a template literal to dynamically construct a personalized welcome message for the user. These features contribute to cleaner, more expressive code and enhance the developer experience when working with JavaScript.

6.3 Destructuring and Spread/Rest Operators:

Destructuring, introduced in ECMAScript 6 (ES6), is a powerful feature that simplifies the process of extracting values from arrays or objects and assigning them to variables. It provides a concise and intuitive syntax for unpacking values, making code more readable and expressive. With destructuring, developers can extract specific properties from objects or elements from arrays directly into variables, eliminating the need for manual assignment.

Here's an example demonstrating destructuring with an object:

```
// Destructuring example
const person = { name: 'John', age: 30 };
const { name, age } = person;

console.log(name); // Output: John
console.log(age);  // Output: 30
```

In this example, the name and age variables are assigned the corresponding values from the person object using destructuring syntax, resulting in cleaner and more concise code.

The spread operator (...) and rest operator (...) are also introduced in ES6, providing convenient syntax for working with arrays and objects.

The spread operator allows for easy copying, merging, and spreading of array elements or object properties. It creates a shallow copy of an array or object, making it useful for tasks such as concatenating arrays or merging objects.

Here's an example demonstrating the spread operator with arrays:

```
// Spread operator example
const numbers = [1, 2, 3];
const newNumbers = [...numbers, 4, 5];
```

```
console.log(newNumbers); // Output: [1, 2, 3, 4, 5]
```

In this example, the spread operator ...numbers spreads the elements of the numbers array into the newNumbers array, resulting in a new array containing all the elements from both arrays.

The rest operator, on the other hand, gathers multiple elements into a single array or object. It allows developers to capture an indefinite number of arguments into a single parameter, simplifying function definitions and array destructuring.

Here's an example demonstrating the rest operator with a function:

```
// Rest operator example
const sum = (...args) => {
  return args.reduce((total, num) => total + num, 0);
};
```

```
console.log(sum(1, 2, 3, 4, 5)); // Output: 15
```

In this example, the sum function uses the rest parameter ...args to gather all the arguments passed to the function into a single array, which is then used to calculate the sum of the numbers.

6.4 Classes and Modules:

ES6 (ECMAScript 2015) introduced significant enhancements to JavaScript, including the class syntax and modules, which revolutionized the way developers structure and organize their code.

Classes in JavaScript provide a more structured and intuitive approach to object-oriented programming (OOP). With the class syntax, developers can define blueprints for objects in a cleaner and more familiar way, similar to other programming languages like Java or C#. Classes encapsulate data and behavior, making it easier to manage and maintain complex applications.

Here's an example demonstrating the class syntax in JavaScript:

```javascript
// Class example
class Animal {
  constructor(name) {
    this.name = name;
  }

  speak() {
    console.log(`${this.name} makes a sound.`);
  }
}

const dog = new Animal('Dog');
dog.speak(); // Output: Dog makes a sound.
```

In this example, the Animal class defines a blueprint for creating animal objects with a name property and a speak() method. Instances of the Animal class, such as dog, can then be created using the new keyword.

Modules, another feature introduced in ES6, provide a standardized mechanism for organizing and reusing JavaScript code. Modules allow developers to break down their code into smaller, manageable pieces, known as modules, and export/import functionality between them.

Here's an example demonstrating modules in JavaScript:

```
// Module example
// Exporting module
export const greet = (name) => {
  return `Hello, ${name}!`;
};

// Importing module
import { greet } from './utils';
```

In this example, the greet function is exported from a module called utils. Other modules can then import this functionality using the import statement. This promotes modularity and code reuse, enabling developers to organize their codebase more effectively and maintain clear dependencies between different parts of the application.

Overall, classes and modules introduced in ES6 have greatly improved the structure, maintainability, and scalability of JavaScript codebases, making it easier for developers to build and maintain complex web applications.;

6.5 New Data Structures: Sets and Maps:

ES6 introduced two powerful built-in data structures to JavaScript: sets and maps. These data structures offer efficient ways to work with collections of data in a variety of scenarios.

Sets are collections of unique values, meaning each value can occur only once within the set. This makes sets particularly useful when dealing with collections where uniqueness is important. Sets provide methods for adding, removing, and checking for the presence of elements, as well as operations like union, intersection, and difference.

Here's an example demonstrating the use of sets in JavaScript:

```
// Set example
const uniqueNumbers = new Set([1, 2, 3, 4, 5]);
uniqueNumbers.add(6); // Adding a new unique number to the set
```

Maps, on the other hand, are collections of key-value pairs, allowing you to associate values with arbitrary keys. This makes maps suitable for tasks where you need to store and retrieve data based on specific identifiers or keys.

Here's an example demonstrating the use of maps in JavaScript:

```
// Map example
const userRoles = new Map();
userRoles.set('John', 'Admin'); // Assigning a role to a user
userRoles.set('Jane', 'User');
```

In this example, the userRoles map associates user names with their respective roles.

Overall, sets and maps provide powerful tools for managing and manipulating data collections in JavaScript, offering efficient methods for common operations and enabling developers to work with data in a more expressive and flexible way.

Throughout this chapter, we've explored various ES6 features and beyond, including arrow functions, template literals, destructuring, spread/rest operators, classes, modules, sets, and maps. These features have significantly enhanced the capabilities of JavaScript, enabling developers to write cleaner, more efficient, and maintainable code..

Chapter 7:
Error Handling and Debugging

Error handling and debugging are critical skills for any JavaScript developer. In this chapter, we'll explore common JavaScript errors, techniques for handling errors effectively using try...catch blocks, various debugging techniques and tools available, and best practices for error handling in JavaScript applications.

7.1 Common JavaScript Errors:

JavaScript, like any programming language, can encounter errors during execution. Understanding common JavaScript errors is essential for debugging and troubleshooting your code effectively. Let's explore some of the most common JavaScript errors and explain them with examples:

1. Syntax Errors:
Syntax errors occur when the JavaScript engine encounters code that violates the language syntax rules. These errors prevent the code from being parsed and executed. Common syntax errors include missing parentheses, semicolons, or curly braces.

```
// Example of a syntax error
var x = 10
console.log(x);
```
In this example, the missing semicolon after var x = 10 results in a syntax error because it violates the expected syntax of JavaScript.

2. Reference Errors:
Reference errors occur when trying to access an undeclared variable or a variable that is not currently in scope.

```
// Example of a reference error
console.log(y); // ReferenceError: y is not defined
```

In this example, trying to log the value of y results in a reference error because y has not been declared or defined anywhere in the code.

3. Type Errors:
Type errors occur when performing operations on values of inappropriate types. This typically happens when trying to call methods or access properties of undefined or null values.

```
// Example of a type error
var x = null;
console.log(x.toUpperCase()); // TypeError: Cannot read property 'toUpperCase' of null
```
In this example, trying to call the toUpperCase() method on null results in a type error because null does not have the toUpperCase() method.

4. Range Errors:
Range errors occur when trying to access or manipulate values that are outside the permissible range, such as accessing an array element with an index that exceeds the array length.

```
// Example of a range error
var arr = [1, 2, 3];
console.log(arr[5]); // RangeError: Index out of range
```
In this example, trying to access arr[5] results in a range error because the index 5 exceeds the length of the array arr.

5. Unhandled Promise Rejections:
Unhandled promise rejections occur when a promise is rejected but no .catch() handler is attached to handle the rejection. This can lead to uncaught promise rejection errors.

```
// Example of an unhandled promise rejection error
```

```javascript
fetch('https://api.example.com/data')
  .then((response) => response.json())
  .then((data) => {
    // Process the data
  });
```

In this example, if the fetch request fails and the promise is rejected, there is no .catch() handler attached to handle the rejection, resulting in an unhandled promise rejection error.

6. Other Runtime Errors:
Other runtime errors can occur due to various reasons, such as trying to call a non-existent function, accessing properties of null or undefined, or attempting to execute code in an inappropriate context.

Understanding these common JavaScript errors and their causes is essential for writing robust and error-free code. By recognizing these errors and learning how to handle them effectively, you can improve the reliability and stability of your JavaScript applications..

7.2 Using try...catch for Error Handling:

In JavaScript, the try...catch statement provides a way to handle exceptions (errors) that occur during code execution. It allows you to gracefully handle errors without interrupting the execution flow of your program. Let's explore how try...catch works and how it can be used for error handling:

1. Syntax:
The try...catch statement consists of two main parts: the try block and the catch block.

```javascript
try {
  // Code that may throw an error
```

```
} catch (error) {
  // Code to handle the error
}
```

2. Using try Block:
The try block contains the code that you want to monitor for errors. If an error occurs within the try block, the execution of the block is halted, and control is passed to the catch block.

3. Using catch Block:
The catch block is where you specify how to handle the error that occurred within the try block. It takes one parameter, error, which represents the error object containing information about the error.

4. Example:
Here's an example of using try...catch for error handling:

```
try {
  // Code that may throw an error
  let result = 10 / 0; // Attempting to divide by zero
  console.log(result); // This line will not be executed if an error occurs
} catch (error) {
  // Code to handle the error
  console.error('An error occurred:', error.message); // Output: An error occurred: Division by zero
}
```

In this example, the try block attempts to divide 10 by 0, which would result in a division by zero error. However, because this operation is within a try block, the error is caught, and the code inside the catch block is executed instead of the program crashing.

5. Nested try...catch Blocks:

You can nest try...catch blocks to handle errors at different levels of code execution. This allows for more granular error handling based on the context of the error.

6. Finaly Block:
Optionally, you can use a finally block after the try...catch blocks. The finally block contains code that is always executed, regardless of whether an error occurred or not. This block is commonly used for cleanup tasks.

```
try {
  // Code that may throw an error
} catch (error) {
  // Code to handle the error
} finally {
  // Code that is always executed
}
```

The try...catch statement is a powerful tool for handling errors in JavaScript. By wrapping potentially error-prone code in a try block and specifying how to handle errors in a catch block, you can create more robust and reliable JavaScript applications. Additionally, the finally block allows for cleanup tasks to be performed regardless of whether an error occurred or not, enhancing the overall error-handling mechanism.

7.3 Debugging Techniques and Tools:
Debugging is a critical aspect of software development, enabling developers to identify and resolve errors, bugs, and unexpected behavior in their code. JavaScript offers a variety of debugging techniques and tools to assist developers in effectively diagnosing and fixing issues. Let's delve into some commonly used debugging techniques and tools, along with examples for each:

1. Console.log() Statements:
Inserting console.log() statements in your code is a straightforward yet powerful debugging technique. It allows you to output values, variables, or messages to the browser's console, providing insights into the state of your code at different execution points.

```
let x = 10;
console.log('Value of x:', x);
```

2. Using Debugger Keyword:
The debugger keyword pauses the execution of JavaScript code and triggers the browser's debugger to inspect variables and expressions. It's useful for analyzing code behavior and identifying issues.

```
let y = 20;
debugger; // Execution pauses here
console.log('Value of y:', y);
```

3. Browser Developer Tools:
Modern web browsers come equipped with powerful developer tools offering various debugging features. These tools include the JavaScript console, debugger, DOM inspector, network monitor, and more.

4. Breakpoints:
Breakpoints allow you to pause code execution at specific lines or statements, facilitating inspection and debugging. You can set breakpoints directly in the browser's developer tools or via debugger statements in your code.

```
let z = 30;
console.log('Value of z:', z); // Breakpoint set here
```

5. Stepping Through Code:

Once execution pauses at a breakpoint, you can step through your code line by line, observing variable changes and execution flow. Stepping options include stepping into, over, and out of functions.

6. Inspecting Variables:
Developer tools enable you to inspect variable values at any point during code execution. You can view variable values in the console, watch variables in the debugger, or hover over variables in your code editor to see their values.

7. Source Maps:
Source maps link minified or transpiled code running in the browser to the original source code. They facilitate debugging by allowing you to debug your code in its original form, even after optimization or transformation.

8. Error Messages and Stack Traces:
When an error occurs, the browser provides detailed error messages and stack traces in the console. These messages help identify the cause of the error and locate the source of the problem in your code.

Mastering debugging techniques and tools is essential for JavaScript developers. By leveraging techniques like console.log() statements, debugger keyword, breakpoints, and browser developer tools, developers can efficiently diagnose and resolve issues in their code, leading to more reliable and robust JavaScript applications.

7.4 Best Practices for Error Handling:

Effective error handling is essential for building robust and reliable JavaScript applications. It helps ensure that your code behaves as expected, handles unexpected situations gracefully, and provides meaningful feedback to users when errors occur. Let's explore some best practices for error handling in JavaScript:

1. Use Descriptive Error Messages:
Provide clear and informative error messages that describe what went wrong and how to resolve the issue. This helps users and developers understand the nature of the error and take appropriate action.

```javascript
try {
  // Code that may throw an error
} catch (error) {
  console.error('An error occurred:', error.message);
}
```

2. Handle Errors Gracefully:
Use try...catch blocks to gracefully handle errors and prevent them from crashing your application. This ensures that your application remains functional even when unexpected errors occur.

```javascript
try {
  // Code that may throw an error
} catch (error) {
  console.error('An error occurred:', error);
}
```

3. Avoid Swallowing Errors:
Be cautious when handling errors to avoid swallowing them unintentionally. Make sure to log or handle errors appropriately so that they are not silently ignored, leading to hidden bugs and unexpected behavior.

```javascript
try {
  // Code that may throw an error
```

```javascript
} catch (error) {
  console.error('An error occurred:', error);
  throw error; // Rethrow the error to propagate it further
}
```

4. Use Specific Error Types:
Use specific error types to differentiate between different types of errors and handle them accordingly. This allows for more precise error handling and better understanding of the error scenarios.

```javascript
try {
  // Code that may throw a specific type of error
} catch (specificError) {
  console.error('Specific error occurred:', specificError);
} catch (error) {
  console.error('An error occurred:', error);
}
```

5. Logging and Monitoring:
Implement logging and monitoring mechanisms to track errors and exceptions in your application. Logging error details, stack traces, and user interactions can help diagnose issues and identify trends over time.

6. Handle Asynchronous Errors:
Handle errors that occur in asynchronous code, such as promises and callbacks, using appropriate error handling techniques. Ensure that promises are properly rejected and callbacks handle errors effectively.

7. Test Error Paths:
Write tests to validate error handling paths in your code. Test for expected error scenarios and ensure that your error handling mechanisms behave as intended under various conditions.

By following these best practices for error handling, you can improve the reliability and stability of your JavaScript applications. Handling errors gracefully, providing descriptive error messages, avoiding error swallowing, using specific error types, and implementing logging and monitoring are key strategies for building robust applications that deliver a seamless user experience.

Error handling and debugging are essential skills for any JavaScript developer. By understanding common JavaScript errors, mastering the use of try...catch for error handling, leveraging debugging techniques and tools effectively, and following best practices for error handling, you can build more robust and reliable JavaScript applications. As you continue your journey in JavaScript development, remember to practice these techniques regularly and strive to continuously improve your debugging skills. Happy coding!

Chapter 8:
Testing and Debugging JavaScript Applications

Testing and debugging are crucial aspects of software development, ensuring that your JavaScript applications function correctly and perform as expected. In this chapter, we'll delve into the importance of testing, how to write unit tests using Jest, various debugging techniques for JavaScript applications, and best practices and strategies for effective testing.

8.1 Introduction to Testing JavaScript Code:

Testing is a crucial aspect of software development, ensuring that your code behaves as expected, meets requirements, and remains reliable over time. In JavaScript development, testing helps catch bugs early, verify functionality, and maintain code quality. Let's delve into an introduction to testing JavaScript code, exploring its importance, types of tests, and popular testing frameworks.

Importance of Testing:
Testing ensures that your JavaScript code functions correctly under various conditions and scenarios.
It helps identify bugs and errors early in the development process, reducing the cost of fixing issues later.
Testing provides confidence in code changes, facilitating code refactoring and maintenance.
It improves code quality, readability, and maintainability by encouraging modular and testable code design.

Types of Tests:
Unit Tests:
Unit tests focus on testing individual units or components of your code in isolation. They verify that each unit behaves as expected and produces the correct output for given inputs.

Unit tests are typically small, fast, and easy to write, making them an essential part of the test suite.
Tools/Frameworks: Jest, Mocha, Jasmine.

Integration Tests:
Integration tests validate interactions between different units or components of your code. They ensure that integrated components work together as intended and handle data flow correctly.
Integration tests help identify issues arising from the integration of multiple units, such as communication errors or data mismatches.
Tools/Frameworks: Cypress, Selenium, Puppeteer.

End-to-End (E2E) Tests:
End-to-end tests validate the entire application workflow from start to finish, simulating real user interactions and scenarios.
E2E tests verify that all components and systems work together seamlessly and meet user requirements.
Tools/Frameworks: Cypress, Selenium, TestCafe.

Snapshot Tests:
Snapshot tests capture the current state of UI components or data structures and compare them against previously saved snapshots. They ensure that UI components render consistently and accurately over time, detecting unintended changes or regressions.
Tools/Frameworks: Jest, Enzyme.

Popular Testing Frameworks:
Jest:
Jest is a powerful testing framework developed by Facebook, known for its simplicity, speed, and built-in features such as mocking and snapshot testing.
It's widely used for writing unit tests, integration tests, and snapshot tests in JavaScript projects.

Jest provides a rich set of assertions, matchers, and utilities for writing and executing tests efficiently.

Mocha:
Mocha is a flexible testing framework that supports various testing styles (e.g., BDD, TDD) and integrates with different assertion libraries and mocking frameworks.
It offers a simple and extensible architecture, allowing developers to customize test suites and reporters according to project requirements.
Mocha is often used in conjunction with other libraries such as Chai for assertions and Sinon for mocking.

Cypress:
Cypress is an end-to-end testing framework designed for testing modern web applications. It provides an interactive test runner, real-time feedback, and automatic waiting for DOM elements.
Cypress simplifies the process of writing, debugging, and running E2E tests, making it ideal for testing complex user interactions and workflows.
It offers built-in features for stubbing, spying, and mocking network requests, as well as taking screenshots and videos during test runs.

Testing JavaScript code is essential for ensuring its correctness, reliability, and maintainability. By incorporating different types of tests, such as unit tests, integration tests, and end-to-end tests, along with popular testing frameworks like Jest, Mocha, and Cypress, developers can build high-quality applications with confidence. Testing not only identifies bugs early but also promotes code quality, fosters collaboration, and enhances overall software development processes..

8.2 Writing Unit Tests with Jest:

Unit testing is a fundamental practice in software development aimed at testing individual units or components of code in isolation. Jest is a popular JavaScript testing framework developed by Facebook, known for its simplicity, speed, and built-in features. In this section, we'll explore how to write unit tests using Jest, including setting up Jest, writing test suites, assertions, and utilizing Jest's powerful features.

Setting Up Jest:
Installation:
Install Jest using npm or yarn in your project's directory:
css
npm install --save-dev jest
or
sql
yarn add --dev jest

Configuration (Optional):
Jest automatically detects and runs test files with names ending in .test.js or .spec.js. You can customize Jest's behavior by adding a jest.config.js file or configuring Jest in your package.json.

Writing Test Suites and Test Cases:
Describe Blocks:
Use describe() blocks to group related test cases (test suites) and provide a description for better organization and readability.

```
describe('Calculator', () => {
  // Test cases go here
});
```

Test Cases:

Write individual test cases using the test() or it() function within describe() blocks. Each test case should focus on testing a specific behavior or functionality of the unit being tested.

```
test('adds 1 + 2 to equal 3', () => {
  expect(sum(1, 2)).toBe(3);
});
```

Assertions and Matchers:
Assertions:
Use assertions to verify expected outcomes or behavior of the code being tested. Jest provides a rich set of assertion functions known as matchers.

```
expect(result).toBe(expected);
expect(array).toHaveLength(length);
expect(object).toHaveProperty(property);
```

Matchers:
Jest's matchers allow you to perform various comparisons and checks on values, objects, arrays, and more.

```
expect(value).toBe(expected); // Strict equality check
expect(array).toContain(value); // Array contains value
expect(object).toMatchObject({ key: value }); // Object matches partial shape
```

Mocking Functions and Dependencies:
Mock Functions:
Use Jest's built-in mocking features to create mock functions and simulate behavior of dependencies or external modules.

```
const mockFunction = jest.fn();
mockFunction.mockReturnValue('mocked value');
```

Mock Modules:
Jest allows you to mock entire modules or specific functions within modules to isolate units under test and control their behavior.

```
jest.mock('./myModule');
```

Running Tests:
Command Line Interface:
Run Jest from the command line to execute tests. Jest will automatically search for and run all test files in your project.

```
npx jest
```

Watch Mode:
Use Jest's watch mode (--watch) to automatically re-run tests whenever files change, facilitating test-driven development (TDD) and iterative development workflows.
css

```
npx jest --watch
```

Writing unit tests with Jest is an essential practice for ensuring code quality, reliability, and maintainability in JavaScript projects. By following Jest's intuitive syntax, utilizing assertions and matchers, and leveraging Jest's mocking capabilities, developers can create comprehensive test suites that verify the correctness and behavior of their code units. With Jest's speed and ease of use, unit testing becomes a seamless part of the development process, leading to more robust and stable software applications.

8.3 Debugging Techniques for JavaScript Applications:

Debugging is a critical skill for developers, allowing them to identify and fix errors or unexpected behavior in their code. In JavaScript development, various techniques and tools can help debug applications effectively. Let's explore some essential debugging techniques for JavaScript applications:

1. Console.log():
Description: Console.log() is one of the simplest and most commonly used debugging techniques in JavaScript. It allows developers to print values, variables, or messages to the browser console.
Usage: Insert console.log() statements at strategic points in your code to track the flow of execution, inspect variable values, or debug conditional statements.
Example:
console.log('Debugging message');
console.log(variableName);

2. Using Breakpoints:
Description: Breakpoints are markers placed in the code that pause execution at specific points, allowing developers to inspect the program state, variables, and call stack.
Usage: Set breakpoints in the browser's developer tools or IDE debugger by clicking on the line number where you want to pause execution. Then, run the code in debug mode to pause at the breakpoints.
Example: Set breakpoints in your code editor or browser developer tools, and then step through the code line by line to observe its behavior.

3. Debugging Tools:
Description: Most modern web browsers come with built-in developer tools that offer powerful debugging features, including console logging, breakpoints, step-through execution, watch expressions, and network inspection.

Usage: Open the developer tools in your browser (usually by pressing F12 or right-clicking and selecting "Inspect") and navigate to the "Console" and "Sources" tabs to access debugging features.
Example: Use the Chrome Developer Tools or Firefox Developer Tools to inspect and debug JavaScript code running in the browser.

4. Using Chrome DevTools:

Description: Chrome DevTools is a comprehensive set of web development tools built into the Google Chrome browser. It offers a wide range of features for debugging JavaScript, analyzing network performance, and optimizing web pages.
Usage: Open Chrome DevTools by right-clicking on a web page and selecting "Inspect," or by pressing F12. Navigate to the "Sources" tab to view and debug JavaScript code.
Example: Use the "Debugger" tab in Chrome DevTools to set breakpoints, step through code, and inspect variables in real-time.

5. Browser Compatibility Tools:

Description: Browser compatibility tools help identify and resolve issues related to cross-browser compatibility, ensuring that JavaScript code behaves consistently across different browsers and devices.
Usage: Use online tools or browser extensions to test JavaScript code in multiple browsers and identify compatibility issues. Consider using polyfills or feature detection techniques to address browser-specific issues.
Example: Tools like BrowserStack, CrossBrowserTesting, or modern.ie provide browser compatibility testing services and resources for JavaScript developers.

Effective debugging is essential for identifying and resolving issues in JavaScript applications. By mastering debugging techniques such as console logging, breakpoints, developer tools, and browser compatibility testing, developers can diagnose and fix errors efficiently, ensuring the reliability and performance of their JavaScript code. Debugging is an iterative process that requires patience, attention to detail, and familiarity with debugging tools and techniques. With practice and experience, developers can become proficient at debugging JavaScript applications and deliver high-quality software solutions..

8.4 Testing Best Practices and Strategies:

Effective testing is crucial for ensuring the reliability, performance, and maintainability of JavaScript applications. By adhering to best practices and strategies, developers can create comprehensive test suites that accurately verify the behavior of their code. Let's explore some key best practices for testing JavaScript applications:

1. Write Descriptive Test Cases:
Description: Write test cases that clearly describe the behavior being tested and the expected outcomes. Use descriptive names for test functions and include comments or annotations to explain the purpose of each test.
Example: Instead of test1() or testCase1(), use descriptive names like shouldCalculateSumCorrectly() or shouldHandleEmptyArrayGracefully().

2. Keep Tests Isolated and Atomic:
Description: Ensure that each test is independent and does not rely on the state or side effects of other tests. Tests should be atomic, focusing on testing a single unit or functionality in isolation.
Example: Avoid sharing state between tests or modifying global variables within tests. Reset state or clean up after each test if necessary.

3. Use Mocks and Stubs:

Description: Use mocking and stubbing techniques to isolate units of code and control external dependencies during testing. Mock external services, APIs, or modules to simulate their behavior and ensure predictable test outcomes.

Example: Mock API requests using libraries like fetch-mock or axios-mock-adapter to simulate server responses and test error handling.

4. Automate Testing:

Description: Automate the execution of tests using continuous integration (CI) tools to ensure that tests are run regularly and consistently. Integrate testing into your development workflow to catch bugs early and maintain code quality.

Example: Use CI/CD platforms like Jenkins, Travis CI, or GitHub Actions to automatically run tests whenever code changes are pushed to the repository.

5. Test Edge Cases:

Description: Write tests to cover edge cases and boundary conditions to ensure that your code behaves correctly under all circumstances. Consider scenarios with invalid inputs, extreme values, or unexpected conditions.

Example: Test edge cases such as empty arrays, null or undefined inputs, maximum or minimum values, and boundary conditions to validate the robustness of your code.

By following these best practices and strategies, you can build a robust testing infrastructure and ensure the reliability and quality of your JavaScript applications. Testing is an iterative process that requires careful planning, thorough coverage, and continuous improvement. With proper testing practices in place, you can confidently deliver high-quality software solutions that meet the needs of your users and stakeholders.

Testing and debugging are essential components of the software development process, enabling you to identify and fix errors and ensure the reliability and quality of your JavaScript applications. By understanding the importance of testing, mastering testing frameworks like Jest, leveraging debugging techniques and tools effectively, and following best practices and strategies for testing, you can build more reliable, maintainable, and high-quality JavaScript applications. As you continue your journey in JavaScript development, remember to prioritize testing and debugging as integral parts of your development workflow. Happy coding!

Chapter 9:
Working with APIs

Application Programming Interfaces (APIs) serve as the bridge between different software applications, enabling them to communicate and interact with each other. APIs define a set of rules and protocols for how software components should interact, allowing developers to access and manipulate data or functionality provided by other applications or services.

APIs come in various forms, including web APIs, which expose endpoints over the internet for accessing data or performing actions remotely, and programming language APIs, which provide libraries or frameworks for interacting with specific functionality or services.

In this chapter, we'll explore how to consume web APIs using JavaScript, focusing on RESTful APIs and common techniques for handling API responses, authentication, and authorization.

9.1 Consuming APIs with JavaScript:

Consuming APIs (Application Programming Interfaces) with JavaScript allows developers to interact with external services or resources, such as web servers, databases, or third-party services, to fetch data or perform actions. This process involves making HTTP requests to API endpoints, receiving responses, and handling data in the client-side JavaScript code.

1. Making HTTP Requests:

Description: To consume an API, developers use HTTP requests to communicate with the API server. JavaScript provides several methods for making HTTP requests, including the fetch() API,

XMLHttpRequest (XHR), and third-party libraries like Axios or jQuery.ajax().

Example: Using the fetch() API to make a GET request to an API endpoint:

```
fetch('https://api.example.com/data')
  .then(response => response.json())
  .then(data => {
    console.log(data); // Process the received data
  })
  .catch(error => {
    console.error('Error:', error);
  });
```

2. Handling Responses:

Description: After sending an HTTP request, the API server responds with data or error messages. JavaScript code must handle these responses appropriately, whether by parsing data, handling errors, or updating the user interface.

Example: Parsing JSON data from the API response and displaying it:

```
fetch('https://api.example.com/data')
  .then(response => response.json())
  .then(data => {
    // Process the received data
    console.log(data);
  })
  .catch(error => {
    // Handle errors
    console.error('Error:', error);
  });
```

3. Asynchronous Nature:

Description: API requests in JavaScript are typically asynchronous, meaning they do not block the execution of other code while waiting for a response. Asynchronous programming techniques, such as callbacks, promises, or async/await, are used to handle API requests and responses gracefully.

Example: Using async/await syntax to fetch data asynchronously:
javascript
Copy code

```javascript
async function fetchData() {
  try {
    const response = await fetch('https://api.example.com/data');
    const data = await response.json();
    console.log(data); // Process the received data
  } catch (error) {
    console.error('Error:', error);
  }
}

fetchData();
```

4. Cross-Origin Resource Sharing (CORS):
Description: When consuming APIs from different origins (domains), developers may encounter Cross-Origin Resource Sharing (CORS) restrictions imposed by browsers. CORS policies determine whether a web application can access resources from a different origin.

Example: Handling CORS issues by configuring the API server to allow requests from specific origins using CORS headers.

5. Authentication and Authorization:
Description: Some APIs require authentication or authorization to access protected resources. Developers must include authentication tokens, API keys, or credentials in their requests to authenticate with the API server.

Example: Including an API key or token in the request headers to authenticate with the API server.

By understanding and implementing these concepts, developers can effectively consume APIs with JavaScript, enabling powerful interactions with external services and data sources in web applications.

<h2 align="center">9.2 RESTful APIs and AJAX:</h2>

RESTful APIs (Representational State Transfer) are a popular architectural style for designing networked applications. They use standard HTTP methods (GET, POST, PUT, DELETE) to perform CRUD (Create, Read, Update, Delete) operations on resources, and they typically communicate data in JSON or XML format. AJAX (Asynchronous JavaScript and XML) is a technique used to make asynchronous requests to a server from client-side JavaScript, enabling dynamic and interactive web applications without reloading the entire page.

1. Understanding RESTful APIs:

Description: RESTful APIs adhere to the principles of REST, which define a set of guidelines for building scalable, maintainable, and interoperable web services. These APIs expose resources (such as users, products, or articles) as URLs, and clients interact with these resources using standard HTTP methods.

Example: Accessing user data from a RESTful API endpoint:

```
GET /api/users      // Retrieve all users
GET /api/users/:id  // Retrieve a specific user by ID
POST /api/users     // Create a new user
PUT /api/users/:id  // Update an existing user by ID
DELETE /api/users/:id  // Delete a user by ID
```

2. AJAX (Asynchronous JavaScript and XML):

Description: AJAX is a technique that allows client-side JavaScript code to make asynchronous HTTP requests to the server without reloading the entire web page. This enables dynamic updates, interactive user interfaces, and improved performance by fetching data in the background.
Example: Making an AJAX request to retrieve data from a server:

```
// Using XMLHttpRequest (XHR) object
var xhr = new XMLHttpRequest();
xhr.open('GET', '/api/data', true);
xhr.onreadystatechange = function () {
  if (xhr.readyState === 4 && xhr.status === 200) {
    var data = JSON.parse(xhr.responseText);
    console.log(data); // Process the received data
  }
};
xhr.send();
```

3. Handling Responses:
Description: After making an AJAX request, the server responds with data, typically in JSON or XML format. JavaScript code must handle these responses appropriately, parsing data and updating the user interface as needed.
Example: Processing JSON data received from a server response:

```
var xhr = new XMLHttpRequest();
xhr.open('GET', '/api/data', true);
xhr.onreadystatechange = function () {
  if (xhr.readyState === 4 && xhr.status === 200) {
    var data = JSON.parse(xhr.responseText);
    console.log(data); // Process the received data
  }
};
xhr.send();
```

4. Cross-Origin Resource Sharing (CORS):
Description: When making AJAX requests to a different origin (domain), developers may encounter Cross-Origin Resource Sharing (CORS) restrictions imposed by browsers. CORS policies determine whether a web application can access resources from a different origin.
Example: Handling CORS issues by configuring the server to include appropriate CORS headers in responses to allow requests from specific origins.

5. Security Considerations:
Description: When using AJAX to communicate with a server, developers must consider security aspects such as protecting against Cross-Site Request Forgery (CSRF) attacks, validating and sanitizing input data, and ensuring secure communication over HTTPS.
Example: Implementing CSRF protection mechanisms, input validation, and secure authentication mechanisms to safeguard the application from security vulnerabilities.
By understanding and effectively utilizing RESTful APIs and AJAX, developers can build modern, interactive web applications that communicate with servers asynchronously, retrieve and manipulate data dynamically, and provide seamless user experiences.

9.3 Handling API Responses:

Handling API responses is a crucial aspect of consuming APIs with JavaScript. After making a request to an API endpoint, the server responds with data or error messages, which must be processed and handled appropriately in the client-side JavaScript code. This involves parsing the response data, checking for errors, and updating the user interface based on the received information.

1. Parsing Response Data:
Description: API responses are typically returned in JSON (JavaScript Object Notation) or XML format. JavaScript code must parse the response data to extract relevant information that can be used in the application.
Example: Parsing JSON data received from an API response:

```javascript
fetch('https://api.example.com/data')
  .then(response => response.json())
  .then(data => {
   // Process the received data
    console.log(data);
  })
  .catch(error => {
   // Handle errors
    console.error('Error:', error);
  });
```

2. Checking for Errors:
Description: API responses may include error messages or status codes indicating the success or failure of the request. JavaScript code must check for such errors and handle them gracefully to provide feedback to the user or take appropriate actions.
Example: Checking for errors in the API response status:

```javascript
fetch('https://api.example.com/data')
  .then(response => {
   if (!response.ok) {
      throw new Error('Network response was not ok');
   }
   return response.json();
  })
  .then(data => {
   // Process the received data
    console.log(data);
```

```javascript
  })
  .catch(error => {
   // Handle errors
    console.error('Error:', error);
  });
```

3. Updating the User Interface:
Description: After receiving and processing the API response data, JavaScript code must update the user interface (UI) to reflect the changes or display the retrieved information to the user.
Example: Updating the UI with data retrieved from the API:

```javascript
fetch('https://api.example.com/data')
  .then(response => response.json())
  .then(data => {
    // Update the UI with the received data
    document.getElementById('output').textContent = data.message;
  })
  .catch(error => {
   // Handle errors
    console.error('Error:', error);
  });
```

4. Handling Asynchronous Nature:
Description: API requests and responses in JavaScript are asynchronous, meaning they do not block the execution of other code. JavaScript code must handle API responses asynchronously using promises, async/await, or callback functions.
Example: Using async/await syntax to handle API responses asynchronously:

```javascript
async function fetchData() {
  try {
```

```javascript
  const response = await fetch('https://api.example.com/data');
  const data = await response.json();
  console.log(data); // Process the received data
 } catch (error) {
  console.error('Error:', error);
 }
}

fetchData();
```

By effectively handling API responses in JavaScript, developers can ensure that their applications interact with external services seamlessly, provide accurate feedback to users, and deliver a smooth user experience.

9.4 Authentication and Authorization:

Handling API responses is a crucial aspect of consuming APIs with JavaScript. After making a request to an API endpoint, the server responds with data or error messages, which must be processed and handled appropriately in the client-side JavaScript code. This involves parsing the response data, checking for errors, and updating the user interface based on the received information.

1. Parsing Response Data:
When working with APIs in JavaScript, it's common to receive responses in JSON (JavaScript Object Notation) or XML format. Parsing these responses allows you to extract meaningful information that can be used in your application. Parsing JSON is especially prevalent due to its simplicity and ease of use in JavaScript.

How Parsing Works:
JSON Format: JSON is a lightweight data interchange format that is easy for humans to read and write and easy for machines to parse

and generate. It consists of key-value pairs and arrays, representing objects and lists, respectively.

Parsing Process: To parse JSON data in JavaScript, you typically use the .json() method provided by the Response object returned by the fetch API or other HTTP request libraries. This method converts the raw JSON response into a JavaScript object that you can work with in your code.
Example:

```javascript
fetch('https://api.example.com/data')
  .then(response => response.json()) // Parse JSON response
  .then(data => {
    // Process the received data
    console.log(data);
  })
  .catch(error => {
    // Handle errors
    console.error('Error:', error);
  });
```

In this example:
We make a fetch request to the specified API endpoint.
We use the .json() method on the response object to parse the JSON data.
The parsed data is passed to the second .then() block, where we can access and process it.
Any errors during the request or parsing process are caught and handled in the .catch() block.

Benefits of Parsing:
Data Extraction: Parsing allows you to extract specific pieces of data from the API response that are relevant to your application's functionality.

Data Manipulation: Once parsed, you can manipulate the data as needed, such as displaying it in the user interface, performing calculations, or storing it for later use.

Error Handling: Parsing helps in identifying errors or inconsistencies in the response data, allowing you to handle them appropriately.

Considerations:

Error Handling: Always handle errors that may occur during the parsing process, such as invalid JSON format or network issues.

Data Structure: Understand the structure of the JSON data returned by the API to effectively parse and utilize it in your application.

By parsing API responses effectively, you can integrate external data seamlessly into your JavaScript applications, enabling dynamic and interactive experiences for users.

2. Checking for Errors:

When working with APIs in JavaScript, it's important to check for errors in the response to ensure that your application behaves correctly and provides appropriate feedback to users. Errors can occur due to various reasons, such as network issues, server errors, or invalid data format. Checking for errors allows you to handle these situations gracefully and provide meaningful error messages to users.

Why Check for Errors:

Robustness: Checking for errors ensures that your application can handle unexpected situations without crashing or behaving unpredictably.

User Experience: Providing clear error messages helps users understand and troubleshoot issues, improving their overall experience with your application.

Error Recovery: Handling errors gracefully allows your application to recover from failures and continue functioning smoothly.

How to Check for Errors:

Response Status: Most HTTP responses include a status code that indicates the success or failure of the request. Common status codes include 200 for success, 404 for not found, and 500 for server errors.

Response Body: In addition to the status code, the response body may contain additional information about the error, such as error messages or error codes.

Error Handling: Use the .catch() method to catch any errors that occur during the request or parsing process and handle them appropriately.

Example:

```javascript
fetch('https://api.example.com/data')
  .then(response => {
   if (!response.ok) {
     throw new Error('Network response was not ok');
   }
   return response.json();
  })
  .then(data => {
   // Process the received data
   console.log(data);
  })
  .catch(error => {
   // Handle errors
   console.error('Error:', error);
  });
```

In this example:

We make a fetch request to the specified API endpoint.
We check the ok property of the response object to determine if the request was successful. If not, we throw an error with a descriptive message.

If the request was successful, we parse the JSON data and proceed with processing it.
Any errors during the request, parsing, or processing are caught and handled in the .catch() block.

Best Practices:
Provide Context: Include descriptive error messages that explain what went wrong and suggest possible solutions.
Log Errors: Log errors to the console or a logging service for debugging purposes and to monitor application health.
Graceful Recovery: Whenever possible, try to recover from errors and continue executing the application logic.
By checking for errors in API responses, you can ensure that your JavaScript application handles failures gracefully and provides a reliable user experience.

3. Updating the User Interface:
When working with JavaScript and APIs, updating the user interface (UI) is a common task. After fetching data from an API or performing other asynchronous operations, you often need to reflect the changes in the UI to provide feedback to users or display the retrieved information. Updating the UI involves manipulating HTML elements, changing their content, appearance, or structure dynamically based on the data received from the API or user interactions.

Importance of Updating the UI:
Real-Time Feedback: Updating the UI allows you to provide real-time feedback to users, indicating that their actions have been processed or displaying updated information.
Enhanced User Experience: Dynamic UI updates create a more engaging and interactive experience for users, improving the overall usability of your application.

Visual Representation: Displaying data visually through the UI helps users understand and interpret the information more effectively.

How to Update the UI:
Select DOM Elements: Use JavaScript to select the HTML elements in the DOM (Document Object Model) that you want to update. This can be done using methods like document.getElementById(), document.querySelector(), or document.querySelectorAll().
Update Element Content: Modify the content of selected elements by changing their innerHTML, textContent, or other relevant properties.
Modify Element Styles: Adjust the appearance of elements by changing their CSS styles using the style property or by adding/removing CSS classes.
Create New Elements: Dynamically create new HTML elements using the createElement() method and append them to the DOM as needed.
Remove Elements: Remove existing elements from the DOM using methods like removeChild() or remove().
Example:
Html code

```html
<!DOCTYPE html>
<html lang="en">
<head>
  <meta charset="UTF-8">
  <meta name="viewport" content="width=device-width, initial-scale=1.0">
  <title>Dynamic UI Update</title>
  <style>
    .container {
      text-align: center;
    }
  </style>
</head>
```

```html
<body>
  <div class="container">
    <h1>Welcome, <span id="username"></span>!</h1>
    <button id="fetchBtn">Fetch Data</button>
    <div id="dataContainer"></div>
  </div>

  <script>
    // Select elements
    const usernameElement = document.getElementById('username');
    const dataContainer = document.getElementById('dataContainer');
    const fetchBtn = document.getElementById('fetchBtn');

    // Event listener for fetch button
    fetchBtn.addEventListener('click', fetchData);

    // Function to fetch data from API
    function fetchData() {
      // Simulated API call
      setTimeout(() => {
        const data = 'Lorem ipsum dolor sit amet, consectetur adipiscing elit.';
        // Update UI with fetched data
        dataContainer.textContent = data;
      }, 1000);
    }
  </script>
</body>
</html>
```

Best Practices:

Keep it Responsive: Ensure that UI updates are performed efficiently to maintain smooth performance, especially in large-scale applications.

Provide Feedback: Use loading spinners, progress bars, or other visual cues to indicate to users that data is being fetched or the UI is being updated.

Accessibility: Ensure that UI updates do not hinder accessibility features such as screen readers and keyboard navigation.

Error Handling: Implement error handling mechanisms to gracefully handle errors that may occur during UI updates, such as failed API requests or invalid data responses.

By effectively updating the UI in response to API data or user interactions, you can create dynamic and responsive web applications that provide an engaging user experience.

4. Handling Asynchronous Nature:

In JavaScript, handling asynchronous operations is a common requirement, especially when working with APIs, fetching data from servers, or performing time-consuming tasks. Asynchronous operations allow your code to continue executing while waiting for tasks such as network requests or file I/O to complete. Properly managing asynchronous behavior is crucial for building responsive and efficient applications.

Why Handle Asynchronous Nature:

Responsiveness: Asynchronous operations prevent blocking the main thread, ensuring that your application remains responsive and doesn't freeze during long-running tasks.

Efficiency: By executing tasks asynchronously, you can optimize resource utilization and improve overall application performance.

Concurrency: Asynchronous programming enables concurrent execution of multiple tasks, allowing your application to perform tasks in parallel when possible.

How to Handle Asynchronous Nature:

Promises: Use promises to represent asynchronous operations and handle their results or errors asynchronously. Promises provide a clean and intuitive way to work with asynchronous code and simplify error handling.

Async/Await: Async/await is a modern JavaScript feature that allows you to write asynchronous code in a synchronous style using async functions and the await keyword. Async/await simplifies asynchronous code by making it look and behave like synchronous code, making it easier to understand and maintain.

Callback Functions: Callback functions are a traditional approach to handling asynchronous operations in JavaScript. While they are still widely used, they can lead to callback hell and make code difficult to read and maintain, especially with deeply nested callbacks.

Example:

```javascript
async function fetchData(url) {
  try {
    const response = await fetch(url); // Perform asynchronous fetch request
    if (!response.ok) {
      throw new Error('Failed to fetch data');
    }
    const data = await response.json(); // Parse JSON response asynchronously
    updateUI(data); // Update the user interface with the fetched data
  } catch (error) {
    console.error('Error:', error); // Handle any errors that occur during the fetch operation
  }
}
```

In this example:

We define an asynchronous function fetchData that takes a URL as a parameter.
Inside the function, we use the await keyword to perform an asynchronous fetch request to the specified URL.
We check if the response is successful using the ok property of the response object. If not, we throw an error.
We use the await keyword again to parse the JSON response asynchronously.
Finally, we call the updateUI function to update the user interface with the fetched data.

Best Practices:
Error Handling: Always handle errors gracefully using try/catch blocks or .catch() methods to prevent unhandled exceptions.
Avoid Callback Hell: Use modern asynchronous patterns such as promises and async/await to avoid nested callback functions and improve code readability.
Optimize Performance: Consider asynchronous optimizations such as parallelism, batching, and caching to improve application performance.
By effectively handling the asynchronous nature of JavaScript, you can build responsive, efficient, and maintainable applications that provide a seamless user experience.

Working with APIs is a fundamental skill for web developers, enabling them to access and integrate data or functionality from external services into their applications. By understanding the principles of APIs, mastering techniques for consuming APIs with JavaScript, and learning how to handle API responses, authentication, and authorization effectively, developers can build powerful and dynamic web applications that interact seamlessly with external services. As you continue your journey in web development, remember to explore and experiment with different APIs to expand your skills and create innovative applications.

Chapter 10:
JavaScript Frameworks and Libraries

JavaScript frameworks are pre-written JavaScript code libraries or tools that provide developers with a structured way to build web applications. These frameworks offer a set of guidelines, conventions, and reusable components to streamline the development process and ensure consistency and maintainability across projects.

Frameworks abstract common tasks and patterns, such as DOM manipulation, state management, and routing, allowing developers to focus on building features rather than writing boilerplate code. By leveraging frameworks, developers can build complex and scalable web applications more efficiently.

Overview of React, Angular, and Vue.js:

React, Angular, and Vue.js stand out as three of the most widely used JavaScript frameworks for constructing contemporary web applications. Each possesses unique characteristics, strengths, and applications, rendering them suitable for varying project scopes and developer inclinations.

React: Spearheaded by Facebook, React represents a declarative, component-based library crafted for crafting user interfaces. Its virtual DOM implementation and unidirectional data flow render it exceptionally efficient for constructing dynamic and interactive web applications. React's allure stems from its adaptability, performance, and extensive ecosystem of supplementary libraries and tools.

Angular: Engineered by Google, Angular emerges as a comprehensive, all-encompassing framework tailored for erecting large-scale web applications. Offering an array of potent tools for constructing single-page applications (SPAs), Angular features two-way data binding, dependency injection, and an extensive suite of built-in directives and components. Angular's opinionated nature and comprehensive feature set make it well-suited for enterprise-grade projects with intricate requirements.

Vue.js: Conceived by Evan You, Vue.js stands as a progressive JavaScript framework geared towards crafting user interfaces. Revered for its simplicity, ease of integration, and adaptability, Vue.js presents a progressive adoption model, permitting developers to gradually incorporate it into existing projects. Vue.js's reactive system, component-based architecture, and intuitive API position it as a stellar option for constructing contemporary web applications of any magnitude..

Choosing the Right Framework for Your Project:

When faced with the decision of selecting a JavaScript framework for your project, it becomes imperative to take into account various factors to ensure a successful outcome. Key considerations include project specifications, team proficiency, performance metrics, and community assistance.

React: Opting for React proves advantageous when flexibility, performance enhancements, and an extensive array of third-party libraries and tools are paramount. Its virtual DOM implementation and unidirectional data flow architecture contribute to heightened efficiency, making it an apt choice for projects necessitating dynamic and interactive interfaces.

Angular: Projects with substantial scale and intricate requisites find Angular to be an apt selection. Boasting robust built-in features, support for two-way data binding, dependency injection, and a multitude of pre-built directives and components, Angular excels in managing large-scale applications and facilitating enterprise-level development.

Vue.js: Vue.js emerges as the framework of choice for endeavors prioritizing simplicity, seamless integration, and a progressive development approach. Its incremental adoption model allows for smooth integration into existing projects, while its reactive system, component-based structure, and intuitive API streamline the process of crafting modern web applications.

Ultimately, the decision rests upon aligning the unique demands of your project with the strengths and capabilities of each framework. React shines in scenarios demanding adaptability and performance, Angular excels in handling complex requirements and large-scale deployments, while Vue.js thrives in projects emphasizing simplicity and ease of adoption.

Integrating JavaScript Libraries:

In tandem with JavaScript frameworks, developers frequently incorporate JavaScript libraries to augment functionality and expand the capabilities of their applications. These libraries furnish reusable code snippets, utilities, and components, simplifying the development process and fostering efficiency.

Among the plethora of JavaScript libraries utilized in web development, several stand out for their widespread adoption and utility:

Axios: This library facilitates streamlined handling of HTTP requests, offering a concise and intuitive API for making asynchronous calls to web servers. Axios simplifies tasks such as fetching data from APIs and handling responses, making it a staple in modern web development projects.

Moment.js: Recognized for its comprehensive suite of features for date and time manipulation, Moment.js empowers developers to effortlessly parse, validate, manipulate, and display dates and times in various formats. Its extensive functionality makes it indispensable for tasks involving temporal data.

Lodash: Renowned for its vast assortment of utility functions, Lodash streamlines common programming tasks by providing a rich set of methods for array manipulation, object manipulation, data transformation, and functional programming paradigms. Its modular design enables developers to selectively incorporate only the functionalities they require, optimizing resource usage.

jQuery: Although its prominence has waned in recent years with the advent of modern JavaScript frameworks, jQuery remains a prevalent choice for DOM manipulation and traversal. Its concise syntax and cross-browser compatibility simplify tasks such as selecting elements, manipulating CSS styles, handling events, and executing AJAX requests.

Integrating JavaScript libraries into projects entails straightforward procedures, typically involving the inclusion of the library's script file in the HTML document or installation via package managers like npm or yarn. Once integrated, developers can harness the library's functionality by invoking its methods and APIs within their codebase, thereby enhancing productivity and expediting development workflows..

Pros and Cons of Using Frameworks:

While JavaScript frameworks offer many benefits, they also come with trade-offs that developers should consider when choosing whether to use them in their projects.

Pros:

1. Productivity: Frameworks provide a structured architecture and reusable components, allowing developers to build applications more quickly and efficiently.

2. Maintainability: Frameworks enforce best practices and conventions, making it easier to maintain and scale applications over time.

3. Community and Ecosystem: Frameworks have active communities and vibrant ecosystems of third-party libraries, tools, and resources, providing support and solutions to common problems.

4. Performance Optimization: Frameworks like React and Vue.js utilize virtual DOM and efficient rendering techniques to optimize performance and minimize re-renders.

5. Developer Experience: Frameworks often come with developer-friendly features such as hot reloading, code splitting, and debugging tools, enhancing the developer experience and productivity.

Cons:

1. Learning Curve: Frameworks have a learning curve, especially for developers new to the ecosystem, requiring time and effort to master their concepts and conventions.

2. Overhead: Frameworks add overhead to applications in terms of bundle size, performance, and complexity, which may impact page load times and user experience.

3. Opinions and Constraints: Frameworks impose their own opinions and constraints on developers, limiting flexibility and requiring adherence to specific patterns and conventions.

4. Migration and Compatibility: Frameworks evolve over time, leading to potential issues with backward compatibility and migration when upgrading to newer versions.

5. Lock-in: Using a framework may result in vendor lock-in, making it difficult to switch to alternative solutions or migrate to different frameworks in the future.

JavaScript frameworks and libraries are indispensable tools for modern web development, offering developers the structure, productivity, and flexibility needed to build dynamic and scalable web applications. By understanding the strengths, weaknesses, and use cases of frameworks like React, Angular, and Vue.js, as well as integrating JavaScript libraries effectively, developers can create innovative and impactful applications that meet the needs of users and businesses alike. As you continue your journey in web development, consider the unique requirements and constraints of your projects and choose the right framework and tools that best align with your goals and priorities. Happy coding!

Conclusion

JavaScript is a versatile and powerful programming language that has become indispensable in modern web development. Through the exploration of various chapters in this book, we've covered a wide range of topics, from the basics of JavaScript syntax and data structures to advanced concepts such as asynchronous programming, error handling, and working with APIs.

We've delved into the importance of understanding fundamental concepts like variables, functions, and control flow, and we've explored the ecosystem of tools, frameworks, and libraries that empower developers to build sophisticated and dynamic web applications.

We've discussed the role of JavaScript frameworks like React, Angular, and Vue.js in simplifying and enhancing the development process, as well as the benefits and trade-offs associated with using frameworks and libraries.

Additionally, we've examined essential techniques for testing and debugging JavaScript code, ensuring the reliability and stability of applications, and enabling developers to identify and resolve issues efficiently.

As you continue your journey in JavaScript development, remember to keep learning, experimenting, and staying up-to-date with the latest trends and technologies. Embrace challenges as opportunities for growth, and never hesitate to seek out resources, communities, and mentors to support you along the way.

With dedication, practice, and a passion for learning, you have the power to unlock endless possibilities and create extraordinary experiences on the web. Thank you for joining us on this journey, and we wish you continued success and fulfillment in your endeavors as a JavaScript developer. Happy coding!